FEELING GOOD ABOUT me

For Brownie – EB
For Wendy and Roy – LP

Written by Ellen Bailey and
Lesley Pemberton
Illustrated by Harry Briggs

Edited by Frances Evans
Designed by Zoe Bradley
Cover designed by Angie Allison

FEELING GOOD ABOUT me

Buster Books

First published in Great Britain in 2021 by Buster Books, an imprint of
Michael O'Mara Books Limited, 9 Lion Yard, Tremadoc Road, London SW4 7NQ

 www.mombooks.com/buster   Buster Books   @BusterBooks   @buster_books

ISBN: 978-1-78055-739-7

1 3 5 7 9 10 8 6 4 2

This book was printed in June 2021 by Shenzhen Wing King
Tong Paper Products Co. Ltd., Shenzhen, Guangdong, China.

Contents

Welcome!

This book is all about YOU and how you feel.

It's completely normal to feel lots of different emotions. Sometimes you might feel happy, confident or excited, and sometimes scared, angry or anxious. Sometimes you may feel all these things at once! Your emotions, thoughts and dreams are all part of what makes you wonderful and unique.

These pages provide a fun, friendly space to help you think about and record your thoughts and feelings. You might find that when you do this you feel some big or confusing emotions. Who could you talk to if this happens? Perhaps you could even invite someone you trust to do the activities with you? You can also ask an adult if there are any words or ideas you come across that you don't recognize.

You can record your thoughts and feelings within these pages in whatever way you want — there are no right or wrong answers. This is your book to enjoy and make your own.

7

"I don't want other people to decide who I am. I want to decide that for myself."

EMMA WATSON
ACTOR & ACTIVIST

This is Me

Write down some things about you and what makes you feel good.

Name: ....

Age: ....

Who I live with: ....

Where I go to school: ....

I feel good about myself when ...	I feel confident doing ...
I am good at ...	I take care of myself by ...

How Do You Feel Today?

Colour in any of the words that describe the way you feel today, or write down some of your own in the empty shapes. It's not right or wrong to feel any of these emotions, and it's possible to feel more than one emotion at the same time.

Imaginative

Relaxed

Enthusiastic

Happy

Sad

Worried

Bored

Calm

Cross

Angry

Excited

Sensitive

Argumentative

Confident

Embarrassed

Pick one of the emotions you're feeling. Can you think about what has happened to make you feel this way? Write a sentence or two about it here.

10

Feeling Different

It may sometimes seem like you have **no control** over the way you feel. But, just as we all look **unique** on the outside, the way we feel about things can be very different.

Here's an example ... Billy, Yasmin and Sameera all send a text to Rafe asking if he'd like to meet up. Rafe doesn't reply to any of them, and they all have **different emotions** about this.

Billy feels hurt. He thinks, "Rafe doesn't like me. I don't think he wants to be my friend anymore."

Yasmin feels anxious. She thinks, "Maybe something bad has happened to Rafe that means he can't reply. I hope he's OK."

Sameera feels relaxed. She thinks, "Rafe's probably busy – I'm sure he'll text back when he's got time."

It's often not the things that happen to us that make us feel the way we do, but the **thoughts and beliefs** that we have about these things.

Look at the sentence you wrote on the opposite page. Can you imagine different emotions other people might feel in the same situation? How might you look at the same situation **differently**?

Take Charge

In addition to feeling emotions, we all think thoughts. Sometimes, having lots of thoughts or very strong thoughts can feel overwhelming, but you can take charge of which thoughts you listen to.

Max is thinking about his spelling test tomorrow. He has the gloomy thought that he's rubbish at spelling and should give up any hope of getting the questions right. But he also has the bright thought that if he practises his spellings today, he's more likely to do well in the test.

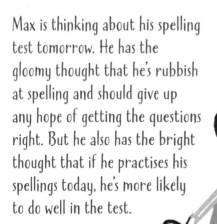

The things that we say to ourselves can make our worries grow or shrink, and the thought that Max listens to will affect the way that he feels and the choices he makes. Like Max, you can take charge of your thoughts.

Try this thought experiment. Imagine you see some kids in the park — it looks like they are having fun and you'd love to join in. Draw a picture of yourself between the two thought bubbles and look at the examples of two very different thoughts you might have.

They might not like me. What if they won't let me join in?

All I have to do is ask. If they won't let me join in, that's OK — I'll just find something else to do.

If you listened to the gloomy thought, how might you feel? You might decide not to ask if you can join in and then you might miss out and feel even worse! What might you do differently if you listened to the positive thought?

13

Thought Bubbles

On the previous page, you read about taking charge of your thoughts. When you feel worried about something, use these thought bubbles to record your gloomy thoughts and bright thoughts. Remember that you can choose which thoughts you pay attention to, and this can change how you feel and what you do.

15

Mindful Moment

Take a moment to colour this calming pattern.

Take Five

Feeling stressed? Use this breathing technique to help you relax ... all you need are your five fingers.

1. Place the tip of the index finger of your right hand at the bottom of your left hand's thumb.

2. Trace your index finger up around the outside of your thumb towards the top, breathing in slowly as you do.

3. When you reach the top of your thumb, pause, then breathe out slowly as you trace down the inside of your thumb.

4. Now trace your finger up the side of your left index finger until you reach the top, breathing in slowly as you do.

5. When you reach the top of your index finger, pause, then breathe out slowly as you trace down the other side.

6. Continue breathing in and out as you trace up and down each of your fingers, pausing at the top. Repeat on the other hand if needed.

This is a great one to do at school. If you're feeling stressed in class, you can trace your hand under your desk to help you feel calmer and more relaxed.

Change the Story

Tunde has been working on a science project for school. He's made an amazing papier-mâché volcano that can erupt. It's the night before he presents it to the class and he's putting the final touches to the volcano when he knocks a pot of paint all over it. Disaster! Or is it? Read Tunde's story below and then see if you can think of some different thoughts, so he has an easier time.

Is this true? Read the introduction about Tunde. Can you think of something more helpful he could say to himself?

Everyone sometimes make mistakes. What could Tunde say to make himself feel better?

Do you think the class will mind that the volcano has paint on it? Give Tunde a helpful thought in the bubble below to make him feel calm and confident.

Shaken Up

When you get too much of one emotion it can feel overwhelming and, just like a shaken-up fizzy drink, you can explode! You might feel like you suddenly get angry or worried, but our emotions usually start small with a few little bubbles and build up over time.

If you can notice or share your emotions when they're small bubbles you can help them to pass before they build up. Do you ever bottle your emotions up? Use words or pictures to fill the bottle with these emotions.

Superpowers

Each of these superhero stars stands for a different superpower. Colour in any that you possess! If you could choose just one, which would it be? Are there any you haven't coloured in that you would like to have, and can you think of anything you could do to develop that superpower?

Kindness

Humour

Courage

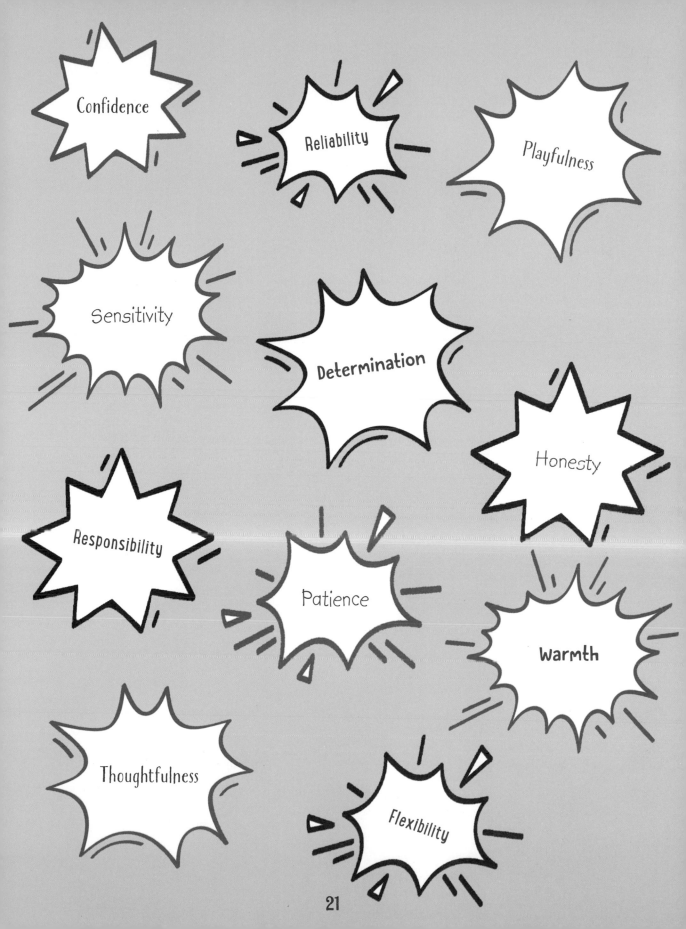

Treasure Chest

This special chest is a place for you to keep your most treasured memories. Fill it with drawings or descriptions of happy times and kind things people have done for you. You could also include positive thoughts you've had about yourself, or times when you've been really proud of something.

Go, Greta!

Greta Thunberg is a young climate activist with Asperger syndrome, and she is changing the world. People with Asperger's see, hear and feel the world differently to other people, and this difference can be a superpower. Read Greta's story below and think about how the world needs all different types of people. Is there something you care passionately about, like Greta?

Age 8: Greta first learns about climate change. Over the next few years, she changes her life so that it has less impact on the planet – she decides to become a vegan and to stop flying on planes.

Age 15: Greta skips school to hold up a sign outside the Swedish parliament that reads "Skolstrejk för Klimatet" ("School Strike for Climate"). At first, she strikes alone, but then other young people start to join her. Word spreads and soon millions of children around the world are striking for the climate. The movement becomes known as "Fridays for Future".

Age 16: The world's media are interested in what Greta has to say, and everyone is impressed with her honest way of speaking. Many world leaders invite her to talk to them about climate change, and she is asked to attend the UN Climate Action Summit in New York. Greta travels across the Atlantic on a zero-emissions yacht.

At the summit, Greta makes a speech that goes viral. She is very angry with the politicians and says: "We are in the beginning of a mass extinction, and all you can talk about is money and fairy tales of eternal economic growth. How dare you!"

Age 17: Greta is nominated for a Nobel Peace Prize and is named *Time* magazine's Person of the Year. She continues to fight for the planet.

Inspirational Interview

Do you know someone in real-life who you think is amazing? Perhaps they do lots of good things for their community, or have a really cool job, or have overcome incredible difficulties. There's lots we can learn from the people we admire, so why not ask them these questions and see what you find out ...

Draw a portrait or stick a photo of the person you're interviewing here.

Name: ....

What is the thing you're most proud of in your life? ....
....
....

What qualities do you have that have helped you achieve your goals? ....
....
....

What advice would you give to someone who wants to be like you? ....
....
....

What were you like when you were my age? ....
....
....

If you could go back in time, what would you tell your younger self? ....
....
....

Is there anything you're scared of? How do you cope with that fear? ....
....
....

What do you do if you make a mistake? ....
....
....

What things do you do to take care of yourself? ....
....
....

What are your dreams for the future? ....
....
....

Do you have ideas for how you are going to make those dreams come true? ....
....
....

Hope Stars

Fill the stars on this page with your hopes and dreams. They can be small, everyday things to focus on in the next week or month, or bigger things that you want to aim for in the future.

Date

Time

Place

2.

1.

3.

4.

....

....

....

....

5.

....

....

....

....

6.

....

....

....

....

7.

....

....

....

....

Journey to Your Dreams

Complete the activity on the previous page, then choose a dream that really excites and motivates you. Going from where you are now to seeing a dream come true is like going on a journey – it needs some planning. Write down the dream you are working towards here, then fill in the gaps below to plan your route: ....

....

1. Packing list
What qualities, skills or knowledge do you already have that will help you make your dream come true? Write them on your packing list on the right.

2. Qualities Shop
Is there a quality that would help you achieve your dream? Perhaps you'd like to be more courageous so you try new things, or more resilient so you can cope with setbacks. Can you think of a way you could develop that quality?

5. Dream Come True
How do you think it will feel when you've achieved your goal?

4. Library of Knowledge
Perhaps your dream is to be the lead in the school play and you need to learn the lines, or you dream of working with animals and you need to learn more about biology. Add titles to these books to sum up the things you'll need to learn to reach your goal.

3. Skills Academy
Are there any skills you need to achieve your dream? Perhaps it's your dream to play tennis and you need to work on your technique, or maybe you want to beat your mum at chess and you're going to practise on the computer. What skills do you need and how are you going to develop them?

"No matter where you're from, your dreams are valid."

LUPITA NYONG'O
ACTOR & AUTHOR

Steps to Success

There are many steps you might go through in the process of achieving a goal. Think of a goal you would like to achieve and write it below. Your goal might be something simple, like learning a times table, or something challenging, like taking part in a park run. Which step are you on at the moment? Colour in that step, and each time you go up a step towards achieving your goal, colour it in, too.

Goal: ....

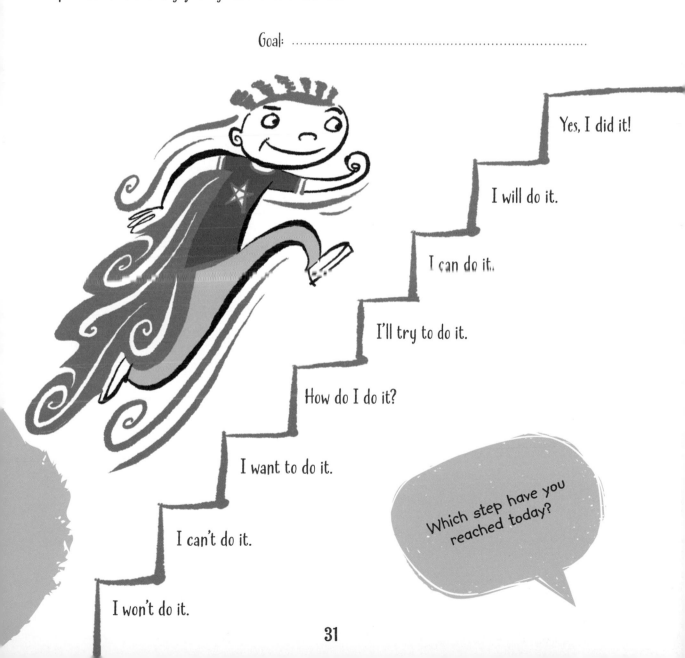

Yes, I did it!

I will do it.

I can do it.

I'll try to do it.

How do I do it?

I want to do it.

Which step have you reached today?

I can't do it.

I won't do it.

31

Tree of Strength

What things in your life make you feel strong? Perhaps there are family members or friends who you can always rely on, or maybe playing sport, listening to music or taking a walk makes you feel invincible. Write the things that give you strength on the leaves of this tree.

Nature Bingo

Spending time in nature feels good! It can improve your health, confidence and self-esteem. Even surrounding yourself with natural objects indoors can help you to feel more relaxed and improve your mood.

How many of the activities on this nature bingo card can you complete? If you complete activities from four boxes all in a row that's bingo ... and if you manage to complete all of them that's a full house!

Walk barefoot on the grass.	Paint a landscape.	Cuddle an animal.	Collect pebbles, leaves or feathers and arrange them in your bedroom.
Plant some seeds in pots and grow them on your windowsill.	Put on your wellies and dance in the rain.	Write a poem about nature.	Listen to the birds.
Make a picture using sticks.	Turn a pebble into a pet using paints and felt-tip pens.	Gaze at the stars.	Use plants, soil and stones to create a mini garden in a glass jar.
Read a book outside.	Climb a tree.	Make friends with a bug.	Fly a kite.

Mindful Moment

Take a moment to colour this beautiful pattern.

Birthday Cake Breathing

When you're feeling too much of one emotion it can help to take some deep breaths to relax your body and mind. This birthday-cake-themed breathing technique is a great way to help you focus on something positive.

1. Hold your hands out in front of you. Imagine that your left hand is a cup full of delicious icing. Hold your hand up to your nose and take a really deep breath in to smell the flavour of the icing. Yum!

2. Now imagine that your right hand is a birthday cake covered in candles. Take your time to blow them out slowly. Keep going until there is no air left in your lungs.

3. Breathing as slowly and deeply as you can, continue breathing in to smell the icing and breathing out to blow the candles.

4. Repeat until you feel calmer.

Celebration Time

Most people celebrate the big things in life, such as birthdays or passing exams, but do you ever take time out to celebrate yourself just the way you are, right here, right now? Here are some ideas for activities you could do. There's also space for you to add your own.

Sing in the shower and marvel at your voice.

Find something you love to do and do it. A lot!

Draw a self-portrait. Get a mirror and take time to really look at yourself and notice all your unique features.

Learn to cook your favourite meal.

....

....

....

When someone pays you a compliment say "thank you" and remember it.

Look at your old baby photos. Think about how amazing it is that you've grown into the person you are today.

Write a poem about yourself where the first letter of each line begins with the letters of your name.

Make a photo collage of you and your friends having fun together.

Put on your favourite song and dance. Admire the way your body moves.

Fill in the award gallery on the next page.

Find your last school report and highlight all the best bits.

....

....

....

....

....

....

Write a letter to your younger self telling them about all the things you have achieved.

Award Gallery

And the award goes to ... you! Award yourself all the trophies in this gallery — simply think of something you've done that's worthy of the award, then write it on the trophy. There are some ideas to inspire you if you can't think of anything — or maybe you could do something today.

PLANET LOVER

CARING FRIEND

TEAM PLAYER

GOOD DECISION
MAKER

HAPPY HELPER

PROBLEM SOLVER

CREATIVE THINKER

GREAT LISTENER

Incredible Vision

Yash Gupta is a young American who has made a huge difference to the lives of tens of thousands of children. Read Yash's story below. What do you particularly admire about Yash? Can you think of a kind act — big or small — that you could do for someone today?

Yash has poor eyesight and has worn glasses from the age of five. One day he was sparring in a taekwondo class when his glasses broke. He was able to order a new pair, but it was going to take a while for them to be made, so he had to go to school without his glasses for a week. This made school so hard! He couldn't focus or learn, and he couldn't see his friends and teachers properly. Yash realized how important his glasses were to his education.

It got him wondering ... how many children in the world need glasses but aren't able to get them? He did some research and discovered that there are millions of children in this situation. Yash also knew that, in America, millions of glasses are thrown away each year.

At the age of 14, Yash set up a charity called Sight Learning. The charity collects glasses from people who don't want them any more, and sends them to students around the world who need them. Sight Learning has now collected and distributed more that 60,000 pairs of used glasses to children in Mexico, Honduras, Haiti and India. Go, Yash!

Coat of Arms

In medieval times, each noble family had its own 'coat of arms' that was painted on to a shield. The coat of arms was special to that family, and had pictures on it of things they valued. Design your own coat of arms by filling this shield with things that are important to you. You could include your hobbies, the people you love, your favourite foods, or just patterns or colours that make you feel good.

Fight, Flight, Freeze

Have you ever noticed changes that happen in your body when you're feeling frightened? Your heart pumps fast, your breathing becomes shallow, and your hands get cold and clammy. Know the feeling? That's your fight, flight, freeze response, and it evolved to keep you safe in dangerous situations.

Survival Mode

Imagine you're a caveman minding your own business. Suddenly, you spot a bear. Before you can even think about it your body goes into **survival mode** and releases hormones called **adrenaline** and **cortisol**. These hormones make you feel alert and prepare you for action so that you can either ...

1. Fight the bear (fight)
2. Run away from the bear (flight)
3. Stay very, very still so the bear doesn't notice you (freeze)

Whichever option you choose, your **fight, flight, freeze response** has kicked in. The reason your heart rate and breathing have increased is to help get oxygen to your muscles quickly. Blood is diverted to your muscles from your hands, feet and digestive system – you don't need to be digesting dinner right now, you need to be dealing with the bear! You start sweating to avoid overheating. You are **ready for action**, and it works – you make it back safely to your cave. You survive to create more humans, who will inherit this brilliant survival response.

You Just Don't Need It

The trouble is that because the response kicks in without you thinking about it, it can happen when you **don't need it**.

It's probably not that often that you need to defend yourself from a bear. Instead, your response might kick in when you have an **exam** or are about to perform in the **school play**. In these situations, you don't need to fight anyone, run anywhere or freeze, but your body might respond as if you do.

In Control

There are things you can do to get your body under control if your fight, flight, freeze response is triggered unnecessarily:

1. Notice it has happened. Turn the page to explore how it feels when your survival response is triggered.

2. Take a breath. Focusing on your **breathing** to make it slow and deep can help send a message to your brain that it doesn't need to be in survival mode. There are all sorts of breathing exercises in this book that you can try out. If you practise the breathing exercises when you're not feeling frightened it will be easier to use them when you are in a **stressful situation**.

Body Map

Read the information on the previous page, then look at the person below – do you recognize any of these responses from when your own fight, flight, freeze response is triggered? Circle the feelings you've experienced.

Feeling dizzy

Feeling sweaty

Racing thoughts

Difficulty concentrating

Fast and shallow breathing

Wanting to run away

Feeling restless

Inability to move

Tunnel vision

Difficulty recognizing people's expressions

Dry mouth

Difficulty swallowing

Racing heart

Cold hands and feet

Butterflies in stomach

Feeling sick

Tense muscles

Needing a wee

Trembling or shaking

Legs like jelly

Can you think of a time when your own fight, flight, freeze response was triggered? Write about how it felt for you in the spaces below.

Where were you?

....

....

....

....

What made you feel frightened?

....

....

....

....

Look at the sensations on the opposite page. Did you notice any of these in your body? Can you map how you felt and where you felt it on the outline on the right?

....

....

....

....

Did your fight, flight, freeze response help you in this situation? What techniques did you use to get your body back under control?

....

....

....

....

Chill Challenge

Need to take some time out to calm down, relax your body and focus your thoughts? Here are some ideas ...

Count backwards from 100.

Blow bubbles.

Do a yoga pose.

Colour in a calming pattern.

Trace a drawing.

Do a breathing exercise — you can find ideas throughout this book.

Roll a piece of playdough into a cube, a ball or a really long snake.

Get a glass of water and drink it really slowly.

Push hard on a wall for 10 seconds, take a break, then do it again.

Hug someone for 20 seconds (ask them first!).

Sort objects into colours or sizes.

Lie on the floor and place your legs up on a chair or sofa.

Mindful Moment

Take a moment to colour this calming pattern.

Colour Your Emotions

Colours mean different things to different people. Think about what feelings each of these colours remind you of and write your ideas in the paint splats. Which colour (or colours) are you feeling today? There are some ideas around the splats to get you started.

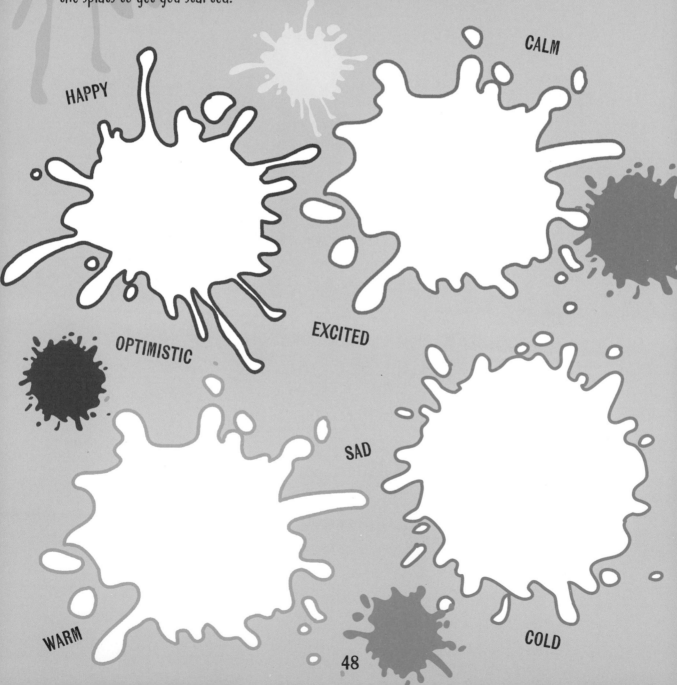

HAPPY

CALM

OPTIMISTIC

EXCITED

SAD

WARM

COLD

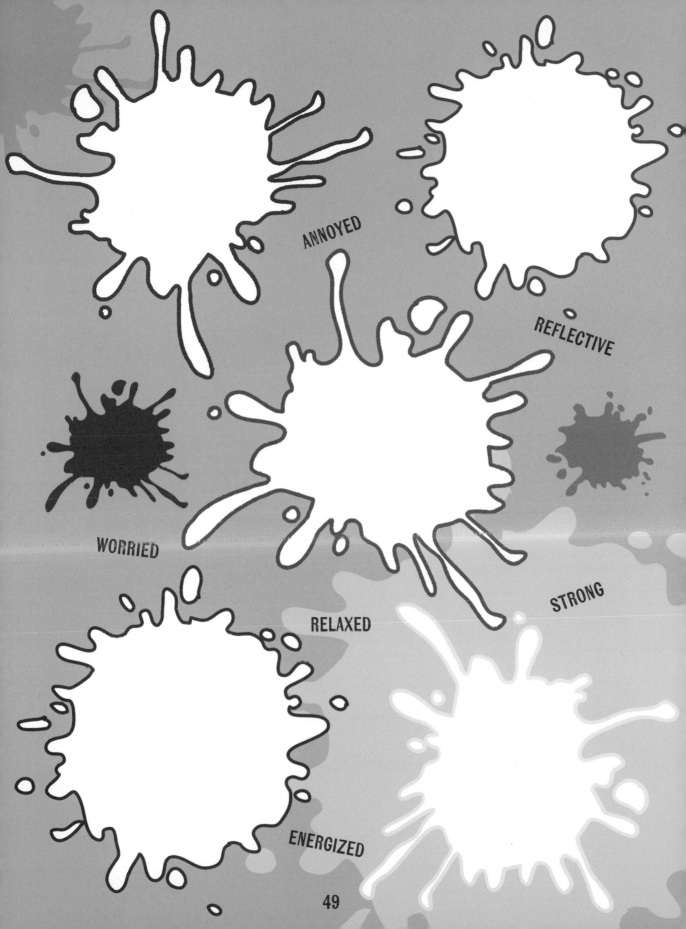

ANNOYED

REFLECTIVE

WORRIED

RELAXED

STRONG

ENERGIZED

49

The Art of Colour

Artists use colour to affect the mood of a picture. Can you think of a famous artwork, or take a look at an example online or in an art book? Study the picture and then have a think about the following questions.

What is the name of the painting and who painted it?

....

....

....

....

How does the painting make you feel?

....

....

....

....

What mood do you think the artist was trying to get across when they painted it?

....

....

....

....

Now use this empty frame to create your own moody masterpiece!

Different is Beautiful

Here are five balls that can be used for sports. Some friends have been asked which one they think is the odd one out. Who do you agree with?

"It's the table-tennis ball because it's light and the others are heavy," says May.

"It's the golf ball because it's the only one that isn't bouncy," says Jasper.

"I think it's the rugby ball because the others are all spheres," says Amira.

Correct!

Whichever answer you chose, you're right. All of these balls are different and are used in different ways. They all have unique qualities ... just like people. And in the same way that different sports need different balls, the world needs all different kinds of people.

Celebrate Your Differences

Draw a picture of yourself and of one of your friends in the spaces left and right below. In the space where the circles overlap, draw the things that you have in common. Perhaps you're both good at dancing, or you both love dogs. In your circle, write some things that are unique to you, and in your friend's circle, write some things that are unique to them.

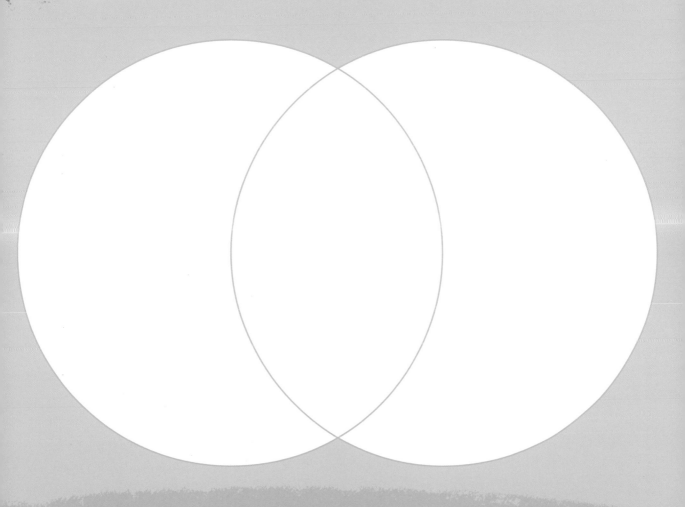

Champion!

Swimming sensation Ellie Simmonds is a British Paralympian. Ellie has always believed in herself and knows she can do anything anybody else can do. Once you've read her story, think about a challenge you'd like to have a go at – then go out there and smash it!

Ellie is a champion swimmer who made a huge splash when she won her first Paralympic medal aged just 13. She was born with a condition called achondroplasia, a type of dwarfism, which means that her arms and legs are short compared to the rest of her body.

Ellie became interested in swimming when she was five years old and it wasn't long before she started swimming competitively. Her determination and drive shone through from the start and led to her being selected for the British squad at the 2008 Paralympics, where she won two gold medals.

In recognition of her achievements, Ellie was made an MBE (Member of the Order of the British Empire) by Queen Elizabeth II – at the age of 14, she was the youngest person to ever receive the award. She went on to repeat her success at the London 2012 Paralympics, winning four medals: two golds, a silver and a bronze.

Today, Ellie balances her training with charity work. She is an ambassador for WaterAid and The Scout Association, and patron of the Dwarf Sports Association, a charity that helps people of restricted growth get into sport.

Things I Love

Someone once said that sometimes the smallest things take up the most room in your heart. What are the things that fill your heart with joy? Write one thing you love in each of the pieces of this heart.

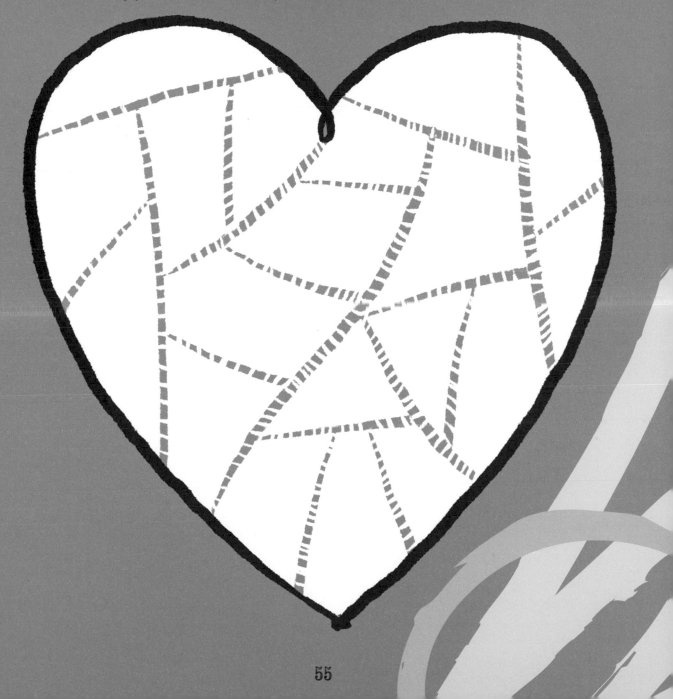

"Friendship is not something you learn in school ... but if you haven't learned the meaning of friendship, you really haven't learned anything."

MUHAMMAD ALI
BOXER & ACTIVIST

Circles of Support

Sometimes we all need some extra support in our lives. Where can you turn to get the support that you need? Write or draw your ideas in the circles of support below.

People who support you, such as friends and family

Things you can do to take care of yourself, such as going for a walk or listening to music

Places you can go for support, such as after-school clubs

What Makes a Good Friend?

Are you a good friend? And can you spot when someone isn't being a good friend? Look at each of these scenarios and write down which person you'd most like to be friends with. What would you do in each of these situations? What do you think your friends would do?

1. Good friends listen

Luca arrives late to school covered in mud. He wants to tell his friends what happened.

… Alva gives Luca her full attention and listens without interrupting.

… Tate jumps in and tells a story about a time he got covered in mud.

… Leo rolls his eyes at Luca and heads to the classroom without waiting to hear what happened.

....

....

2. Good friends are trustworthy

Elise confides in her friends that she doesn't know how to tell the time – she's embarrassed and doesn't want anyone to know.

… Zara bursts out laughing but says she'll keep it a secret.

… Amelia reassures her it's OK and offers to help her learn.

… Cerys tells everyone in the class and invents a new nickname for Elise.

....

....

58

3. Good friends make you feel good

Aisha beats all her friends in a race.

... Florence scowls at Aisha and doesn't speak to her for the rest of the day.

... Tulsi smiles at Aisha and says, "You only beat me because I got a stitch."

... Rana claps her on the back in a friendly way and says, "Great job!"

....

....

4. Good friends support you

Mac is feeling down because his brother has gone away on school camp for a week.

... Beto stays away from Mac until he's feeling happier.

... Sofia notices that Mac is missing his brother and asks if he'd like to come to
     her house after school.

... Jake tries to make him feel better by listing all the things that are annoying about
     Mac's brother.

....

....

5. Good friends allow you to have different interests

Frances has discovered a new singer that she absolutely loves, but none of her friends like them.

... Fred thinks it's great that Frances has found some new music she's into and is happy to
     spend some time doing different things.

... Luis thinks it's ridiculous that Frances is into that singer and finds someone else to be friends with.

... Jamie laughs at Frances for liking the singer and tries to get her into a singer that he really likes.

....

....

....

Friendship Gallery

Fill the frames with pictures of your friends. If you have just one or two close friends you can fill the frames with lots of different drawings of the same people. Underneath each frame write the name of the friend you've drawn and one thing you love about them.

....

....

....

....

What Would You Do?

There are lots of different ways to solve friendship problems — you just need to choose the right key to open the door to friendship peace. Choose a key to open each of the doors below and draw a line to connect them. If you want to, you can use the same key more than once.

APOLOGIZE

SHARE

You're meant to be going to your friend's house this afternoon but you've got a last-minute invitation to a birthday party that sounds amazing.

You've got one beanbag and you and your friend both want to sit on it.

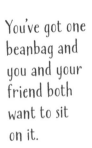

You had a really tough morning and when your friend tried to talk to you, you yelled at them. Now you feel bad.

COMPROMISE

GET HELP

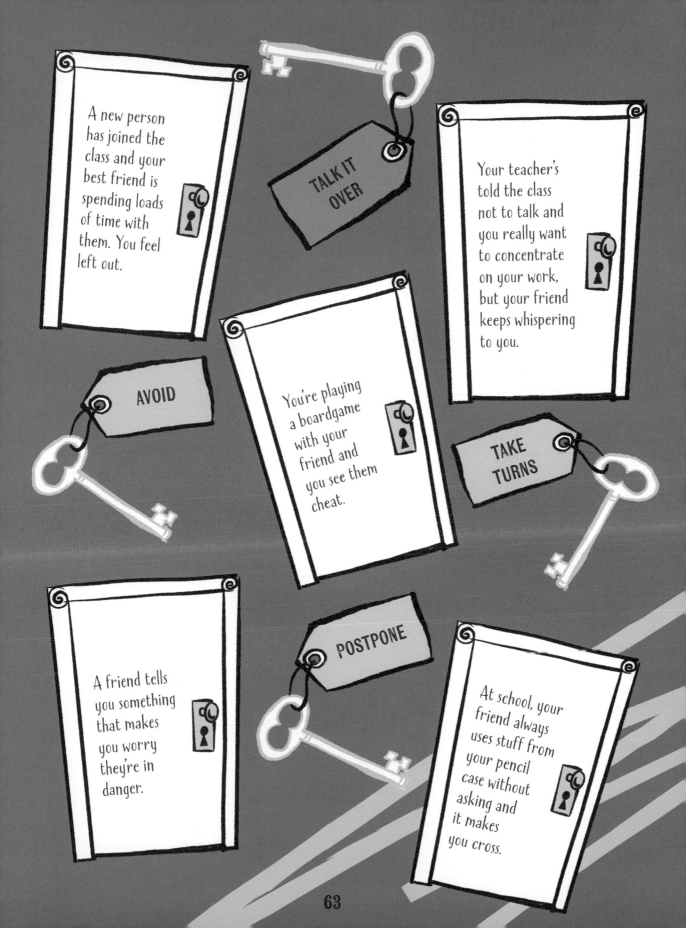

A new person has joined the class and your best friend is spending loads of time with them. You feel left out.

TALK IT OVER

Your teacher's told the class not to talk and you really want to concentrate on your work, but your friend keeps whispering to you.

AVOID

You're playing a boardgame with your friend and you see them cheat.

TAKE TURNS

A friend tells you something that makes you worry they're in danger.

POSTPONE

At school, your friend always uses stuff from your pencil case without asking and it makes you cross.

63

Pizza Massage

Massage can decrease stress levels, increase your ability to concentrate, and help you sleep better. You can do this easy pizza massage on your own hand, or you could team up with a friend and take it in turns to deliver the best pizza ever!

1. If you're doing this with a friend, ask them to put their hand flat on a table, with the palm facing down.

2. Check that your friend is happy for you to give them a hand massage.

3. Start by making the pizza base. Use your fist to gently press their hand. Check with your friend that they're comfortable with it, and ask if they'd like you to do it more firmly or more gently.

4. Stretch out the dough. Rest the palm of your hand on their hand, and move your hand in a circular motion.

5. Make the dough into a pizza shape. Use the tip of your finger to trace a circle on the back of their hand.

6. Add the tomato sauce. Make your hand into a cup shape and move it in small circles all over their hand.

7. Sprinkle on the cheese. Tap your fingertips all over your friend's hand.

8. Ask them what toppings they'd like. Make up your own gentle massage moves to match the toppings.

9. When you've finished, swap over and order your own pizza!

Laughter Milkshake

Laughing can help to release tension and make you feel good, so whenever you're feeling stressed out, why not mix up your very own laughter milkshake?

1. First, imagine that you're holding a milkshake cup. Make it a big one.

2. Next, think of some things that really make you laugh. They could be jokes, or funny things that have happened, or even things you've seen online that have made you laugh. Think of the times you've laughed until your sides ache. Imagine putting each of these things into your milkshake glass. Feel free to have a giggle as you add them.

3. Next, shake up all the funny things together. Take a big gulp of your imaginary milkshake and feel your laughter start to grow. Drink the whole milkshake and let the laughter take over your body. Laugh and laugh and laugh some more!

4. Mix up a laughter milkshake whenever you're in need of a good laugh.

Say What?

Do you ever struggle to know what to say? Words are powerful. It's important to choose your words carefully and think about how the things you say might help or hurt your friendships. Read the sentences below and put a tick next to the ones that you think would be helpful, and a cross next to the ones that you think would be hurtful. With the hurtful sentences, can you think of something that you could say instead?

I know I can trust you. ☐

I am way better than you at art. ☐

☐ You're more fun than anyone I know ... including bubble wrap!

My backpack is better than yours. ☐

Ava told me a secret and I promised not to tell you. ☐

☐ Let's be friends forever!

You're a terrible singer, right? ☐

My mum says I can only have three people to my birthday party so you can't come. □

You don't need more friends – you have me! □

You would be so much cooler if you gelled your hair. □

Why are you frightened of water? Look at me dive straight in! □

Congratulations on getting the part in the play – you deserve it! □

□ I know you can do it.

□ Would you like to share these strawberries with me?

I'm so glad I met you. □

□ Wow, you are clever – I wish I could be that smart.

Your jokes are the best! □

Friendship High-Fives

Bring some sunshine into the lives of your friends with these friendship high-fives —
one act for each finger of your hand. How many acts of kindness can you complete?

Older and Younger Friends High-Five

1. Read a story to a friend who is younger than you.
2. Help a younger friend with their homework.
3. Ask an elderly friend about what life was like when they were young.
4. Offer to help an elderly friend with jobs around the home.
5. Introduce your older and younger friends to your schoolfriends.

Faraway Friend High-Five

1. Post your friend a packet of their favourite sweets.
2. Record a video message for your friend.
3. Draw a picture of your friend and send it to them in a homemade frame.
4. Call your friend and tell them how much they mean to you.
5. Send your friend a postcard.

Best Friend High-Five

1. Let your friend have a turn before you.
2. Make a bookmark and secretly leave it in your friend's book.
3. Teach your friend a new game or skill.
4. Write a nice message in chalk on the pavement outside your friend's front door.
5. Celebrate your friend's successes.

New Friend High-Five

1. Sit next to someone new at lunch.
2. Ask someone who is alone if they'd like to do something together.
3. Learn a magic trick and amaze a new friend.
4. Pay someone a compliment.
5. Share a smile with someone.

Being Resilient

Imagine a tree that is firmly rooted in the ground. In a storm, the tree is pelted with raindrops and it bends and sways in the wind, but it does not break. The tree is resilient.

Being resilient doesn't mean pretending that difficult situations – or storms – don't happen in our lives. It means getting through the storms and staying strong.

Above the umbrellas on this page are five skills that can help you in situations where you need to be resilient. Decorate each of the umbrellas, and think about your own resilience in the face of a storm. Which of these skills are you already good at and which would you like to develop?

1. Letting go physically: using sport and physical activities to let go of emotions

2. Optimism: looking on the bright side and believing that the storm will pass

3. Letting go mentally: using techniques to let go of unhelpful thoughts and worries

4. Self-awareness: the ability to know yourself and name your feelings

5. Attention: being present in the moment and developing mindfulness

71

The Bright Side

Mo and Helena are both given a glass with the same amount of water in it. Mo looks at his and says, "My glass is half full – great!" while Helena looks at hers and says, "My glass is half empty – urgh!"

Mo is an optimist – he looks on the bright side and feels happy. Helena is a pessimist – in the exact same situation she feels cross and unhappy. How do you tend to look at situations? Rate yourself on this optimism-meter:

When you find yourself in a challenging situation, looking for the good can help you be more resilient. Resilient people tend to find it easier to **bounce back** from problems, so it's worth challenging pessimistic thoughts.

If you rated yourself on the gloomy side of the scale, see if you can get into the habit of looking on the **bright side**, and then come back and try the optimism-meter again.

Shake It Off

Physical exercise can help to release tension and help you let go of difficult thoughts or feelings. Here are some ideas for things you could do that don't need anyone else or any special equipment.

Shake your whole body as if you're a giant wobbly jelly.

Move around your home pretending to be different animals – jump, crawl, do what feels good!

Think of six exercises, then roll a dice to decide which one to do.

Set up an obstacle course and time yourself to complete it.

Put on some music and dance, dance, dance!

Try out the yoga moves on the next page.

73

Yoga

Yoga originated in India about 5,000 years ago and is an important part of the Hindu religion. Today, many people practise a form of yoga that focuses on strength, flexibility and breathing. It can help both your body and your mind to feel good. Have a go at these simple poses. You can try them one at a time or turn them into a five-step routine.

1. Start by standing tall like a tree. Say to yourself: "I am confident."

2. Stretch out as a warrior. Think to yourself: "I am brave."

3. Be a dog. Think to yourself: "I am loving."

4. Be a butterfly. Say to yourself: "I am free."

5. Finish your routine by resting on the beach. Take a slow breath. Think to yourself: "I am relaxed."

Balloon Breathing

In this breathing exercise you are going to pretend to blow up an enormous balloon and then release it into the sky.

1. To begin, put your palms together and hold your hands up in front of your face so that your thumbs are in front of your lips. Imagine you are holding a balloon that's your favourite colour.

5. When the balloon is as big as you can reach, imagine throwing it up into the sky. Watch it fly away into the distance.

2. Take a deep breath in through your nose. Slowly release your breath through your mouth, moving your hands outwards as you do so, as if a balloon was expanding between your palms.

3. At the end of the breath, keep your hands where they are and take another deep breath in through your nose. Again, spread your hands further apart as you exhale.

4. Keep breathing in and out, expanding your hands and imagining the balloon getting bigger and bigger.

"I've learned that people will forget what you said, people will forget what you did, but people will never forget how you made them feel."

MAYA ANGELOU
POET, AUTHOR & ACTIVIST

Who's Your Hero?

Is there someone who you look up to in your life? Think of a person you admire and who you feel you can learn from. It might be someone you live with, someone at school or someone famous.

Draw a picture of your hero in this frame and write their name underneath.

Write a sentence or two here about your hero and why you admire them:

....

....

....

....

What five words best describe your hero?

1. ....

2. ....

3. ....

4. ....

5. ....

What piece of advice do you think your hero would give you?

....

....

....

....

What one thing could you do in the next week to become more like your hero?

....

....

....

....

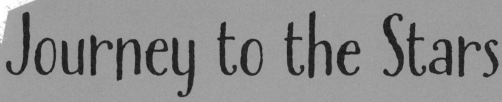

Journey to the Stars

Imagine that you're an astronaut. Soon you will be blasting off into space, leaving your home and travelling far away into the depths of the universe. How do you feel? Excited? Nervous? You're likely to have some big feelings about starting this new phase of your life ... going into space is a huge change! Use these pages to think about the things that could help and support you on your journey.

The space team can fit your craft with messaging devices to five people back on Earth. Who would you like to be able to contact for encouragement and support?

....

....

....

....

....

Fill these photo frames with pictures of things that you'd like to be reminded of about life on Earth.

Write some encouraging words to yourself here. You'll be able to look at these on the spaceship if ever you're feeling wobbly.

....
....
....
....
....
....
....

Is there anything you'd like to take with you to help you feel at home? What would you pack in your suitcase to bring you comfort?

....
....
....
....
....
....

Martian Mayhem

Speaking in a made-up language can help you explore your emotions. Imagine you're an alien from another planet who speaks a language no one on Earth has heard before. There's no right or wrong when you speak alien — you can use all kinds of nonsense words, sounds and signals. Try telling the stories below using your own made-up language. You could talk to yourself in the mirror or find someone else to speak with and take it in turns.

Talk about a time you smelt a really revolting smell.

Talk about something that happened in your day.

Talk about a time something funny happened.

Talk about a time you felt angry.

Talk about a time you felt worried.

Marvellous Mae

Mae Jemison is an American physicist, engineer and former astronaut. In 1992, she was the first African-American woman to travel into space. Read her inspiring story, then think about a dream — big or small — that you have. What do you need to do to achieve it?

When Mae Jemison was a child she loved dinosaurs, adventuring, the stars and space. Mae was an African-American girl, and in the books she read and the programmes she watched about space she couldn't see any astronauts that looked like her. Nonetheless, she dreamed of joining NASA.

At school, Mae was talented at lots of things — she was really good at science, dancing and speaking languages. She could speak English, Russian, Swahili and Japanese!

When she finished school, Mae decided to study chemical engineering at university. She then qualified as a doctor and served as a medical officer in the Peace Corps in West Africa, where she helped to improve healthcare.

Mae always believed in herself, and applied to join NASA's astronaut programme. She succeeded, and became the first African-American woman to go into space.

Mae also believes in young people, and she started an international science camp called The Earth We Share, where students aged 12–16 work to find solutions to the world's problems. Today, she is leading 100 Year Starship — a project to develop travel to other star systems within the next 100 years.

Exploring Empathy

Empathy involves imagining what it's like to be someone else and understanding the way that they feel. The first step in exploring empathy is to think about the fact that people can all feel completely differently about the same thing. To do this, fill in the chart below, filling out your preferences on the first row and then asking three other people to complete the remaining rows.

NAME	FAVOURITE ACTIVITY	FAVOURITE FOOD	FAVOURITE PLACE

Something Special

Do you all feel the same way about activities, food and places? Probably not – we all like different things and feel differently about the world and our experiences.

Choose one of the people who completed the chart and think about doing something special for them.

If you think just about your own preferences you might arrange for the two of you to do your favourite activity together, or make them your favourite food, or take them to your favourite place. This is really kind, but if you use empathy you can do even better! What if your favourite food is something they don't like, or your favourite activity is giving people hugs, but hugs make them feel uncomfortable? If you put yourself in the other person's shoes and think about their favourite activity, food and place, you could organize something that they'd enjoy even more.

Ask a Question

In this example, you asked the person to complete the chart so you knew their answers, but most of the time in life we don't go around asking people to fill in charts about the way they feel. Instead, it can be helpful to check in with people and ask.

You could say something like:
"Would you like to ..."
"Shall we ..."
"Do you mind if ..."
"How do you feel about ..."

Emoji Emotions

Have a look at the scenarios below. How would you feel in each of these situations? For each scenario draw an emoji in the circle that best describes the way you'd feel. Try asking friends or family members how they would feel in these situations. Would they feel differently to you, or the same?

It's reading time.

You've been invited to a friend's birthday party.

You get told off.

You're going on holiday tomorrow.

Your parents or family members are arguing.

You're exercising.

You're playing a video game on your own.

You break something.

You're given a present.

You make a mistake.

You have a maths test today.

You don't understand something.

You're late for school.

Someone in your family is ill, in hospital.

You are going on a trip without your family.

You fall out with your friends.

You're invited to a reptile and insect party.

Your friend is off school.

Mindful Moment

Take a moment to colour this calming pattern.

Relaxometer

What is your energy like today? You probably find that sometimes you're buzzing with excitement and can't keep still, and other times you're cool, calm and completely relaxed. Can you check in with your energy and colour in where you are on this relaxometer?

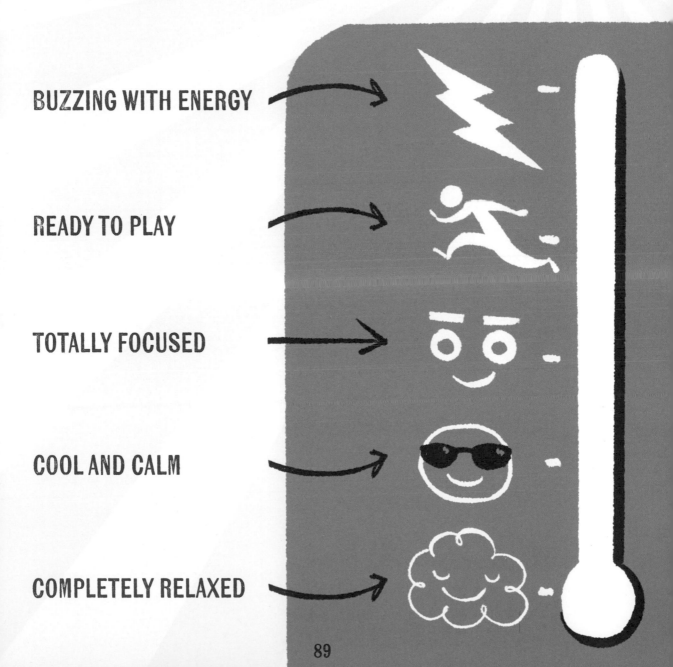

BUZZING WITH ENERGY

READY TO PLAY

TOTALLY FOCUSED

COOL AND CALM

COMPLETELY RELAXED

Postcards From Your Happy Place

Where in the world do you feel your most happy, safe, confident and relaxed? Perhaps on a beach you once went to on holiday, or perhaps in your own cosy bed. Fill these postcards with pictures of your happy places. Next time you're feeling stressed, imagine receiving one of the postcards and picture yourself there. Turn the page for ideas for how to make your happy place come to life in your imagination.

All My Senses

Whenever your spirits need lifting it can help to imagine yourself somewhere you feel good. To help the place feel real in your mind, try remembering it with all of your five senses. Think of your happy place now and write what you can sense there in each of the spaces below.

I CAN SEE ...

....

....

....

I CAN TASTE ...

....

....

....

I CAN HEAR ...

....

....

....

I CAN SMELL ...

....

....

....

I CAN FEEL ...

....

....

....

Hand Soothing

This is a great activity for those times when you feel the
need to practise some mindfulness without anyone noticing.
Waiting your turn to read in front of the class? Feeling nervous?
Want to ground yourself? Try this!

1. Use your right hand to very gently stroke the back of your left hand. Start from your wrist and stroke very, very slowly towards your fingertips.

4. What do your nails feel like? Swap hands and see if you can feel any differences between the two.

2. Pay attention to the texture and notice every bump along the way.

3. What temperature is your hand? Does it feel different at the knuckles?

Nourishing Nature

Spending time in nature can help to improve your mood. The sounds of nature can make you feel calmer, and getting active outdoors can increase your confidence and self-esteem. Here are some ideas you might like to try to connect with nature ... either bringing the natural world into your home or getting out there and immersing yourself in the wild.

Have a sunflower growing competition — whose will grow the tallest?

Press flowers between the pages of a heavy book.

Identify and follow animal tracks.

Look at the Moon at the same time each week. Notice how it changes over a month.

Make a den outside.

Cut different fruits and vegetables in half, dip them into paint, and use them to make prints.

Listen to recordings of natural sounds such as waves or birdsong.

Learn how to do a somersault or cartwheel on the grass.

Go for a walk and count all the birds and insects you spot.

Get up early and watch the sun rise. Listen to the dawn chorus.

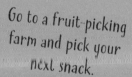

Grow your socks! Wet them, put them on over your shoes, and go for a walk in nature. Put them in a plastic bag and leave them on a sunny windowsill to sprout.

Make an outdoor obstacle course and time yourself to complete it.

Make a tower of pebbles.

Go to a fruit-picking farm and pick your next snack.

Research different types of clouds then go cloudspotting.

Make a bird feeder by covering a pine cone in peanut butter and seeds and hanging it near your window.

Sit or lie down on a patch of grass. Take in the sounds, smells and sights of the natural world around you.

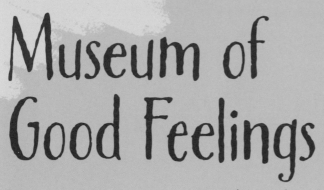

Museum of Good Feelings

Imagine a museum of your favourite things. Write down the things that make you feel happy, joyful, calm, proud, excited and loved inside the objects on these shelves.

My Mantras

Colour and decorate these speech bubbles that contain words of encouragement. Choose one phrase to be your very own mantra, learn it and remember it whenever you need a boost.

I am amazing, I am brave, I am strong.

I believe in myself.

The best way to get something done is to begin.

I am enough.

I can't control what happens to me but I can control how I respond.

I am kind, I am smart, I am important.

This is tough but so am I.

Everything will be all right in the end. If it's not all right, it's not the end.

I have the confidence to be myself.

Mistakes help me grow.

The more I practise, the better I'll get.

Everything is difficult before it is easy.

Let It Go

Fill these boats with your worries, then imagine them drifting off to sea.

You've Got This

Think of something you're having trouble with at the moment. Perhaps it's learning your times tables, or doing a somersault underwater – something that you can't do ... YET! Write your goal on the island. Then, write an encouraging thought on each of the stepping stones that will help you reach your goal. This could be something like "If I keep practising, I know I'll improve" or "I can do hard things".

"If everything was perfect, you would never learn and you would never grow."

BEYONCÉ
SINGER & ACTOR

Making Mistakes

Did you know that making mistakes is a very good thing?

Your brain is full of cells called **neurons**. When you learn new things, the neurons send messages to each other and make new **connections** – you can think of it as building bridges between the cells. Before you've built the bridge, it's hard work to get from one neuron to the other. But once you've built the bridge, it gets stronger every time you cross. That thing that you used to find **difficult** becomes **easy**.

When you make a mistake, your brain grows even more. Mistakes make your neurons spark, and amazingly your brain fires up and grows even if you don't realize you've made a mistake. If you then think about the mistake your brain responds again, this time in a different way.

Every time you make a mistake you get **brainier**, and if you then think about the mistake you get brainier still!

Children and adults everywhere often feel terrible when they make a mistake. This is because they don't realize that mistakes are actually a good thing.

So next time you make a mistake, give yourself a high-five – you just helped your brain to grow!

103

Favourite Mistakes

As well as helping your brain grow, mistakes can result in surprisingly good things. Have you ever made a mistake that's actually worked out even better than the perfect thing you were planning? Take a look at these inventions that were created by mistake.

That Will Do N-icely

Back in 1905, an eleven-year-old boy called Frank Epperson was making a drink on his back doorstep by mixing soda water powder with water. When he went to bed he left it there with the stirrer still in. During the night, the temperature dropped, and when Frank got up in the morning he found the first-ever ice lolly! When he grew up, he turned this mistake into a business. He sold 'Epsicle Ice Pops' in seven different flavours. Later, his children insisted that he change the name to 'popsicles'. Today over 3 million popsicle ice lollies are sold each year.

Super(glue) Powers

Scientist Spencer Silver was given the job of making a super-strong glue. It did not go well. Silver put the glue he'd made on to strips of paper, hoping that they would stick firmly to other surfaces. They didn't. In fact, they could be peeled off any surface! Silver was feeling really down about it until one of his scientist friends pointed out that these little pieces of paper made brilliant, movable bookmarks. The sticky note was born.

Dough!

Playdough was invented by mistake by a soap company that was trying to invent a paste to clean stains off wallpaper. The wallpaper putty they made wasn't very good at cleaning ... but a nursery school teacher who was related to one of the company's workers took it into her classroom for the children to play with. The kids loved it! It was such a hit that the soap company stopped making soap and started making playdough.

Breakfast Blunder

Cornflakes were invented by mistake when the Kellogg brothers forgot about some wheat they had cooked and left to go stale. Not wanting to waste the wheat, the brothers ran it through their bread machine anyway, hoping that it would still turn into dough. What they got instead were flakes, which they toasted and ate for breakfast.

Accidental Art

Mistakes are opportunities for great creativity. Can you turn these splodges, squiggles and scribbles into silly portraits or funny creatures?

Turn It Around

Have you ever made a mistake that you've been able to turn around into something positive? Write the mistake in the long tail of the arrow ... it looked like you were heading towards a problem, right? But then you turned it around. Write or draw what happened next in the head of the arrow. Did things turn out better than you'd planned? Great job!

Mindful Moment

Take a moment to colour this beautiful pattern.

"Being brave isn't the absence of fear. Being brave is having that fear but finding a way through it."

BEAR GRYLLS
ADVENTURER, TV PRESENTER & AUTHOR

Bye Bye, Plastics

In 2013, sisters Melati and Isabel Wijsen felt fearful about the climate crisis they could see unfolding in the world around them. They felt pretty hopeless about it until an inspirational lesson at school encouraged them to tackle their fear and make a difference. Read their story below, then think about something you feel strongly about. What could you do to make a change?

The lesson that made such an impact on Melati and Isabel was about inspirational leaders, such as Nelson Mandela and Mahatma Gandhi. The sisters thought about the saying "be the change you want to see in the world", and decided to do just that!

At just 10 and 12 years old, Melati and Isabel Wijsen set up a non-profit organization called Bye Bye Plastic Bags. Their aim is to make the Indonesian island of Bali where they live plastic-bag free – and then do the same across the rest of the world. Bye Bye Plastic Bags has become an international movement, inspiring people around the globe to act now.

To date, Melati and Isabel have ...

- Worked with a pilot village of 800 families to make it plastic-bag free.

- Spoken to over 20,000 young people, as well as politicians and global leaders, about their mission.

- Launched teams in 25 countries across the globe.

- Created two educational booklets for use in schools. The booklets teach other young people about the harm caused by plastic-bag waste.

- Worked with students to build floating beams called booms from recycled materials. The booms are used to collect plastic bags and other waste from rivers.

Beat It Beach

Problems can feel easier to beat if you break them down into manageable chunks and think about them in different ways. Next time you have a problem, use this beach scene to help you find ways to tackle it and make the Sun come out again!

Write or draw a picture of your problem in this cloud.

What things give you the strength to deal with your problem? Write them on the tree.

What steps could you take to help solve this problem? List them on the surfboard.

What will it be like when your problem is solved? Write it in the Sun.

Problems often have lots of different causes. On each of the waves write down one thing that is causing your problem. Do any of them look easy to address? Surf those waves first!

Describe the ways you have tackled problems before on the towel.

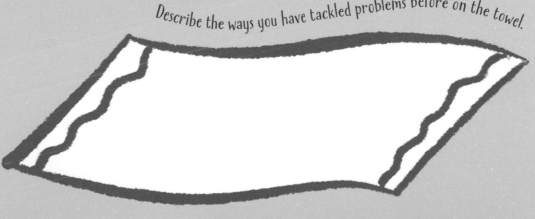

Draw It

Drawing can be a great way to focus on the present. This activity is not about producing a technically brilliant artwork but about enjoying the process, and using drawing as a tool for being in the here and now.

To start, find an object from the natural world that you like. It could be a shell, a flower or a fallen leaf ... anything that helps you feel connected to nature. Put the object in front of you and complete each of the following art challenges.

Draw your object in one minute.

Draw your object in the time it takes to breathe in and out once.

Draw your object in one continuous line without taking your pencil off the paper.

Draw your object
in four lines.

Draw your object
using only dots.

Put your pencil in your other
hand to draw your object.

Draw your object
upside down.

Draw your object
with your eyes shut.

Thank-You Notes

Focusing on the things in your life that you're thankful for can help you to feel a sense of gratitude and appreciation. Colour in the things that you're thankful for, and add some more ideas of your own on the empty envelopes. Tonight, see if you can think of three things from the day that you're thankful for before you go to sleep.

Holidays

Pets

Friends

Hugs

Ice cream

Sports

Music

Books

Laughter

The planet

Creativity

Sleep

School

Self Care

To keep your body and mind healthy you need to take care of yourself. There are lots of different ways to do this. Try out the ideas below, and every time you complete one, record how it made you feel. How many days will it take you to complete them all?

Go for a walk
Date: ....
How it made me feel:

....

Talk with a friend
Date: ....
How it made me feel:

....

Eat something healthy
Date: ....
How it made me feel:

....

Play a game
Date: ....
How it made me feel:

....

Get a good night's sleep
Date: ....
How it made me feel:

....

Drink a large glass of water
Date: ....
How it made me feel:

....

Give yourself a compliment
Date: ....
How it made me feel:

....

Tell someone you love them
Date: ....
How it made me feel:

....

Give someone a hug
Date: ....
How it made me feel:

....

Dance to a song
Date: ....
How it made me feel:

....

5, 4, 3, 2, 1

This grounding technique is easy to remember and can be done without anyone knowing you're doing it – perfect for those times you're in a crowd and want to practise some mindfulness without anyone noticing.

5. First, look around you and name FIVE things you can see.

2. Next, take a deep breath through your nose and name TWO things you can smell.

4. Next, listen hard and name FOUR things you can hear.

1. Finally, name ONE thing you can taste.

3. Now, use your fingers to touch THREE different things. These could be your clothes, the back of your hand or the chair you're sitting on – anything within easy reach.

Past, Present, Future

Imagine that each of these groups of kites represents a different part of your life. On the first group, draw pictures to show what your life was like when you were little. On the second group, draw pictures that represent what your life is like now — where you live, who your friends are and the things you like to do. On the third group, draw pictures of what you hope your future will be like — draw the most wonderful life for yourself that you can possibly imagine.

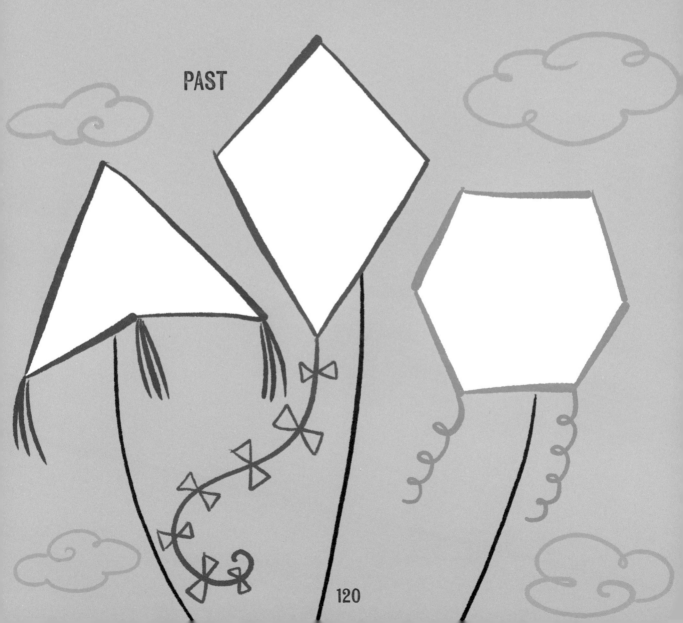

PAST

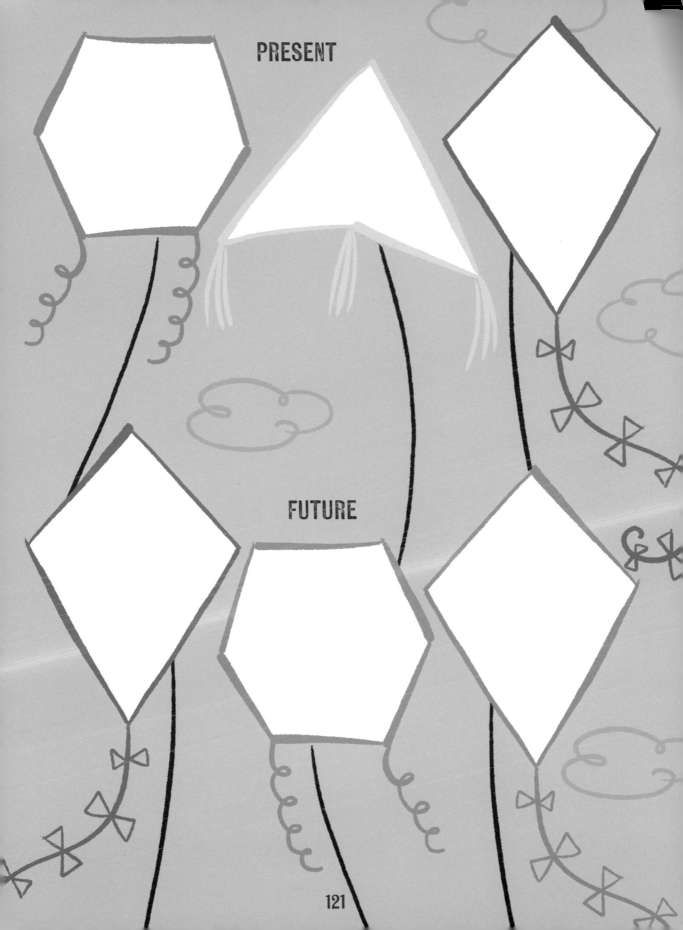

PRESENT

FUTURE

121

Make a Wish

At the end of a long day it can be helpful to think about the things that went well and the things that you hope will be different tomorrow. In each of the shooting stars, write about something you loved about your day. It could be something you achieved, something kind that someone did for you or something delicious that you ate. In the full moon, write something that you would like to achieve or do differently tomorrow.

Sleep Soundly

Getting a good night's sleep is one of the best things you can do to look after your mind and body. Your sleep cycle (the times your body feels ready to go to sleep and wake up) is regulated by a hormone called melatonin. Here are some ways you can signal to yourself that it's time to go to sleep and encourage your body to produce melatonin.

Eat a healthy meal at the same time each evening. This will help to strengthen your internal body clock, and will also stop you waking up in the night because you're hungry or thirsty. Try not to eat too close to bedtime, as it can be tricky to get to sleep if you've just had a big meal.

Avoid screens for an hour before bedtime. The blue light from mobile phones, computers and the TV stops your body producing melatonin effectively. It's best not to have any screens in your bedroom.

Have a warm bath. Make sure it's not too hot, and take some time in there to really relax.

Dim the lights. The darkness will encourage your body to produce melatonin and you'll start to feel sleepy.

Read a book or listen to some gentle music in bed before you go to sleep. You could also think about the things in your day that you feel grateful for.

Breathe. Try breathing in to the count of four and out to the count of eight.

Sweet dreams!

Use the space below to record or draw the things that help you get a good night's sleep. Do you have a favourite book you like to read when you need to unwind, or a song you love to listen to?

Dream Diary

Do you sometimes wake up with a memory of your dream that fades during the day? Keep this book and a pencil by your bed and fill these clouds with words or pictures to describe your dreams as soon as you wake up. Keeping a record of your dreams can help you develop ideas, or reflect on things that are on your mind.

About Blue Smile

Blue Smile is a charity that is dedicated to giving children excellent mental health support. We offer arts-based counselling and therapy to children in schools across Cambridgeshire, and promote a whole-school approach to mental wellbeing. So far, our highly skilled therapists and mentors have helped over 1,200 children to be happier and feel better. We hope that this book helps you to feel good about yourself.

If you need further support, please visit **time-to-change.org.uk**, where you can find an up-to-date list of organizations that can help you.

You can find out more about Blue Smile and ways to support us on our website: **bluesmile.org.uk**

AUSTIN MAHONE
STARTIN' SOMETHING
SPECTACULAR

Mary Boone

TRIUMPH
B O O K S

Triumph Books LLC
814 North Franklin Street
Chicago, Illinois 60610
(312) 337-0747
www.triumphbooks.com

Printed in U.S.A.

ISBN: 978-1-60078-915-1

Content developed and packaged by Rockett Media, Inc.
Written by Mary Boone
Edited by Bob Baker
Design and page production by Patricia Frey
Cover design by Patricia Frey

Photographs courtesy of Getty Images unless otherwise noted.

AUSTIN MAHONE

CHAPTER ONE
FROM TEXAS TO YOUTUBE AND BEYOND

He could have played a video game or read a book. Instead, Austin Mahone battled boredom by posting videos of himself online. He and his best friend, Alex Constancio, started posting videos in June 2010: silly skits, lip-synced music videos, ukulele-backed raps, even clips of them dancing to the hip-hop song "Teach Me How to Dougie."

"We started posting videos because we were bored," Austin told Just Jared in early 2013. "We had nothing better to do, so we started to do that as a hobby, and then it kind of just grew."

And grew and grew and grew.

Six months after posting his first videos, Austin began creating videos of himself singing covers of songs by artists including Justin Bieber, Adele, Bruno Mars and Drake. Thanks to social media, his legion of online fans swelled. His YouTube video covering Bieber's hit "Mistletoe" was posted in October 2011 and has since been viewed nearly 13 million times. In November 2011, even before landing a record deal, Austin debuted at No. 38 on Billboard's Social 50, a chart that combines Web presence and sales. He ranked higher than Demi Lovato, 50 Cent and Jennifer Lopez and just behind R&B diva Beyoncé.

Fast forward to spring 2013 – when Austin begins heading his own tour and joins Taylor Swift as the opening act on her RED tour – and it's clear that this Internet sensation has become a bona fide pop idol in less time than it takes some folks to spell S-U-P-E-R-S-T-A-R.

Austin Carter Mahone was born April 4, 1996, in San Antonio, Texas. His father, Carter Mahone, died when Austin was

> *"I promoted myself on Twitter and Facebook as hard as possible, nonstop,"* [Austin] told **The Hollywood Reporter.** *"People started realizing that if they commented on my videos, I'd reply to their comment, so I started getting a lot more views and comments."*

Austin appears during Y100's Jingle Ball in Ft. Lauderdale, Fla., in December 2012. Photo courtesy of AP Images just 16 months old. An only child, he and his mother, Michele Mahone, moved to the tiny town of La Vernia, Texas (population 1,055), when she remarried.

It was during his La Vernia years that Austin started posting his videos – first comedy, then music. He admits music hasn't always been his thing. Austin had a drum set and messed around with it for a while when he was 6 years old; it wasn't until YouTube commenters offered encouragement that he really began to

get interested in music. His grandfather gave him a guitar and he started taking lessons. His singing, once limited to the shower, improved as it gained a worldwide following.

Uploading music videos is one thing, but Austin wanted to drive traffic to them.

"I promoted myself on Twitter and Facebook as hard as possible, nonstop," he told *The Hollywood Reporter*. "People started realizing that if they commented

Austin and his mom, Michelle, have a tight bond. Photo courtesy of *San Antonio Express-News*

Austin greets fans outside New York's Z100 radio station in June 2012. Photo courtesy of AP Images

Austin poses for photos with fans in Florida. Photo courtesy of AP Images on my videos, I'd reply to their comment, so I started getting a lot more views and comments."

Gurj Bassi, digital director at Universal Music's Republic label, says the fact that Austin has taken the time to respond to fans has likely made a difference in his burgeoning career. "I always try to emphasize this to artists because fans love to have direct contact with the person they idolize, and the Internet makes that possible," said Bassi.

For Austin, that persistence and personal attention has paid off in a big way.

By January 2011, he had 2,000 YouTube fans; a month later, he had attracted 20,000 fans. In March 2011, he was invited to perform at a Playlist.com live concert in Orlando. By May 2013, his YouTube music channel had 802,000 subscribers and his 100-plus videos had attracted a combined 121 million views.

When his mom divorced her second husband, Austin moved back to San Antonio and briefly attended Lady Bird Johnson High School. He'd led a fairly ordinary life up to that point, but it was soon obvious he'd become famous enough that traditional school

Red Cheeked

Think celebrities don't trip, fall off chairs or spill food? Think again.

Austin told the folks at Scholastic's Stacks that his most embarrassing moment came when he was a little kid learning to water ski.

"Somehow my swim trunks like, just came off," he said. "I don't know how it happened. They didn't rip. Like my skis were on, so I don't know how it even happened."

"He wiped out and next thing you know, the skis are upside-down and he's in the water screaming, 'My swim trunks! My swim trunks!'" chimed in Austin's mom, Michelle Mahone. "So I thought for sure they just got torn off of him or something. He still had the skis on his feet, and the swim trunks were gone. We don't know how it happened. They were short skis, you know, because he was like 7 or 8 at the time. And then we saw them floating in the water and we went to get them. I thought they'd be torn, but they weren't. They were totally fine."

wasn't going to work any longer. Girls congregated at his locker, students began taking photos of him during class, and boys became resentful and started hassling him. Within five days, Austin and

MUSIC'S ALIVE IN SAN ANTONIO

Austin Mahone's hometown of San Antonio, Texas, is widely noted for its impressive live music scene and vibrant mix of subcultures.

The city plays host to a wide array of musical acts in small neighborhood bars, outdoor pavilions and entertainment complexes. In addition to the Alamodome, the major concert venues in town include the Verizon Wireless Amphitheater and, when the Spurs aren't playing there, downtown's AT&T Center.

Latin American music and dancing is king in San Antonio's Southtown Arts and Entertainment District. Several clubs there swing to a Cuban, Argentinean, Mexican, or Brazilian beat. First Fridays of the month are the main event in Southtown, when shops, restaurants and clubs stay open late, and special arts events are held.

Hang out in San Antonio for any period of time, and you're likely to hear Conjunto and Tejano music.

Conjunto evolved at the end of the 19th century, when South Texas was swept by a wave of German immigrants who brought with them popular polkas and waltzes. These sounds were easily blended into Mexican folk music. Conjunto music often features the accordion and bajo sexto, a 12-string instrument used for rhythmic bass accompaniment.

Tejano (Spanish for "Texan") is a more modern version of conjunto. The accordion and the bajo sexton are prominent instruments in Tejano, but the music also draws from genres including pop, jazz and country. Conjunto and Tejano gained widespread recognition when Hispanic superstar Selena – who was well on her way to crossover success – was murdered in 1995.

Texas' largest single-day arts event, Luminaria, is held each March in San Antonio's historic downtown. The free showcase features all art forms including dance, literature, media, music, performance and visual arts. More than 315,000 people attended performances at eight stages during Luminaria 2013.

"This annual celebration of the arts has become a hallmark event, showcasing San Antonio as a creative and contemporary hub," San Antonio Mayor Julian Castro said in a news release about the festivities.

San Antonio's nurturing arts environment has yielded dozens of nationally known musicians over the years. A few of the most notable:

CHRISTOPHER CROSS

This singer-songwriter, born Christopher Charles Geppert, first played with a San Antonio-based cover band named Flash before signing a record deal with Warner Bros. He released his debut album, *Christopher Cross*, in 1979; it helped him make Grammy history by winning all four general Grammy awards (Record of the Year, Album of the Year, Song of the Year and Best New Artist) in the same year. That album also won a

Grammy for best musical arrangement for the single "Sailing." Among Cross' biggest hits are the songs "Ride Like the Wind," "Arthur's Theme" (which won the Oscar for Best Original Song in 1981) and "Think of Laura."

HOLLY DUNN

A country artist, Dunn first found fame with her 1986 Top-10 hit "Daddy's Hands." She had more than a dozen singles land on the country music charts, including two No. 1 hits: "Are You Ever Gonna Love Me" and "You Really Had Me Going." Dunn retired from music in 2003 and now works as a painter whose work is exhibited and sold in the southwestern United States.

EMILIO NAVAIRA

An American musician of Mexican descent, Emilio Navaira III (often referred to simply as "Emilio") performs both country and Tejano music. He has charted 10 singles on Billboard Hot Latin Tracks charts and six singles on the Billboard Hot Country Singles & Tracks charts. Emilio has been called the "Garth Brooks of Tejano." The San Antonio-based singer was awarded a 2008 Latin Grammy award for his album *De Nuevo*.

GEORGE STRAIT

This singer and music producer is often referred to as the "King of Country." He rocketed to success after his first single "Unwound" was a hit in 1981 and quickly became known for his unique blend of western swing and honky-tonk. Strait holds the world record for more No. 1 singles than any other artist in the history of music on any chart or in any genre, having recorded 59 number-one hit singles as of 2012. Strait has sold more than 70 million albums in the United States

Emilio Navaira

and his certifications from the RIAA include 13 multi platinum, 33 platinum and 38 gold albums. In the 2000s, he was named Artist of the Decade by the Academy of Country Music and was elected into the Country Music Hall of Fame.

ERNEST TUBB

Nicknamed the "Texas Troubadour," Tubb was one of the pioneers of country music. His biggest career hit song, "Walking the Floor Over You," helped launch the honky tonk style of music. He recorded duets with the then up-and-coming Loretta Lynn in the early 1960s, including their hit "Sweet Thang." Tubb is a member of the Country Music Hall of Fame.

his mother realized that taking online classes at home would be a better option for him.

Austin's Internet fame didn't immediately translate to high-paying record deals and sold out arenas. At first, he played at parties – charging as much as $400 for a 45-minute set – and Skyped with fans for a fee. He sold his own merchandise and performed at PlayList Live, a convention featuring YouTube stars. In late 2012, a Chicago family paid Austin $2,000 to fly in and play at a party. After the performance, the teen singer announced – on very short notice – that he'd meet fans at Chicago's Millennium Park. In what Michelle refers to as a "watershed moment," nearly 1,000 Mahomies (the name he's given his fans) showed up and police had to be summoned to whisk Michelle and Austin away from the riotous crowd.

"That was a turning point," Michelle told *The Hollywood Reporter*, "when I

Austin visits the Empire State Building during a visit to New York City in late 2012.

After appearing on 'Live with Kelly and Michael' in September 2012, Austin took time for photos with fans.

MUSIC, FAME AND THE INTERNET

When Chad Hurley, Steve Chen and Jawed Karim founded YouTube in 2005, they envisioned it as a simple way to upload and share videos with friends. They hoped others would find the website useful, but they couldn't have imagined how incredibly popular it would become. Consider:

• As of April 2013, more than 1 billion unique users visit YouTube each month.

• More than 4 billion hours of video are watched each month on YouTube.

• 72 hours of video are uploaded to YouTube every minute.

• In 2011, YouTube had more than 1 trillion views – equal to approximately 140 views for every person on Earth.

The "discovery" of musician Austin Mahone can be attributed to viral YouTube videos of his performances – a story that's led critics and industry insiders to draw comparisons between him and Justin Bieber.

Austin and JB are definitely YouTube success stories, but they're hardly the first celebs to gain fame via online videos. A few others you may want to check out include:

PSY

Park Jae-Sang, the South Korean rapper better known as Psy, had released six albums before gaining international fame thanks to his catchy hit single "Gangnam Style."

Within the first nine months of its July 15, 2012, release on YouTube, "Gangnam Style" had been viewed more than 1.5 billion times. The song reached No. 1 on the iTunes sales chart and is the most viewed video in the history of YouTube. In 2012, Psy signed with Bieber's manager Scooter Braun and his Schoolboy Records.

ALEX DAY

Described as "one of Britain's most popular YouTubers," Alex Day created his first YouTube channel as a teenager, intent on producing a video podcast to entertain family and friends. He later produced a popular series of humorous videos entitled "Alex Reads *Twilight*," in which

he would read and critically analyze the popular young-adult novel *Twilight*; those videos have received 14 million views.

A talented musician, Day has since released two studio albums, two EPs and had three UK Top 40 hits. As of April 2013, his YouTube channel, nerimon, had nearly 700,000 subscribers; the official video for his single "Good Morning Sunshine" had been watched almost 1.7 million times.

ASHKON

Born to Iranian immigrants in Northern California, Ashkon is a rapper, singer/songwriter and actor. In 2006, Ashkon jumped onto the Bay Area hip-hop scene with his debut record *The Final Breakthrough*.

Two years later, he generated a great deal of buzz with his single "Hot Tubbin' (On the Late Night)." The video for the song became a viral sensation on YouTube, receiving approximately 700,000 views to date, thrusting Ashkon into the national spotlight. Ashkon had another huge Internet hit in 2010, when his San Francisco Giants-related "Don't Stop Believing" YouTube video became the official playoff anthem of the San Francisco Giants and to date has nearly 3 million views.

CHRISTINA GRIMMIE

Christina Grimmie was sitting in math class when she got an unusual text from her brother; he said Selena Gomez's stepfather was trying to contact her. Like thousands of other viewers, Brian Teefey saw her cover of Miley Cyrus' "Party in the U.S.A." on YouTube. It was only her second video on the site (the first was another Cyrus cover, "I Don't Wanna Be Torn"). But

believe it or not, becoming the next big thing wasn't her intention. She told ClevverTV: "It's shocking. I didn't go on YouTube for that. I went on YouTube just to see what would happen and then suddenly things blew up."

And she wasn't exaggerating. With more than 1.5 million subscribers, she became the fourth most subscribed musician on YouTube in May 2012 (as of May 2013, she's closing in on 2 million). She released her debut EP, *Find Me*, in 2011 along with the hit singles "Advice" and "Liar Liar." She's also toured with Selena Gomez, performed at the American Music Awards and has appeared on the *Ellen DeGeneres Show* and the Disney Channel's *So Random!*. She even started her own web series called *Power Up: with Christina Grimmie*.

Although she still doesn't know how she became so popular, Christina has some simple words of advice for anyone trying to be a YouTube star: be unique and ignore the haters.

Austin arrives at Nickelodeon's 26th Annual Kids' Choice Awards in Los Angeles in March 2013.

Austin performs an acoustic song during Y100's Jingle Ball in Ft. Lauderdale, Fla., in December 2012.

started to realize that things were getting crazy."

In the fall of 2012, Austin's mom quit her job as a mortgage loan officer to focus on her son's career.

"We've been through a lot, and we've had a lot of faith that we'd get through it," Michelle said. "I always tell Austin

not to take any of it for granted because the minute you do, it could be gone. We always talk about that – feeling blessed, because he is blessed."

Michelle read books and learned what she could about the music industry. Before long, though, she realized she needed help – things were simply happening too fast.

Michelle and Austin met with dozens of record label executives, producers, managers and songwriters before finally settling on the Miami-based management team at Chase Entertainment. In September 2012, Chase Records announced a deal with Universal Music to conduct distribution, marketing and radio promotions through Universal Republic. The first artist with an album release on the new imprint? None other than Austin!

A statement by Chase Records founders Rocco Valdes, Michael Blumstein and David Abram said: "We are so excited to join the Universal family. Their resources are second to none, their stable of artists is top notch, and their team of executives, A&R and radio reps are the strongest in the industry. We couldn't have asked for a better support system and are excited to have their resources and support to launch Chase Records and the career of teen phenom, Austin Mahone."

That Austin's star is rising doesn't seem to be much of a surprise to industry insiders.

Former American Idol judge Kara DioGuardi told *The Hollywood Reporter* that, in addition to musical talent, fans

Super, Secret Talent

Sure he can sing and dance and play the guitar, but Austin Mahone has talents you may not even know about.

"I can wiggle my ears," he told Scholastic's Stacks. And, as if that wasn't enough, he also has double-jointed thumbs. "I can pull (my thumb back). It looks like I broke it."

Now, *that's* talent.

are drawn to Austin because of his sincerity and openness. "He knows how to connect," she said. "I think people feel attached to him because he's so genuine. He lets (fans) into his bedroom and talks to them in his videos. He's got their notes on the wall ... It's very much what they're going through at that age. When you see him perform, it's like he's singing to you."

An authentic guy who's not putting on airs, who looks you in the eye when he talks to you, who's funny and cute and can sing – not Auto-tune singing, but real, from-the-heart singing? What's not to like about a guy like that? It appears music fans around the world are about to find out for themselves. ★

BREAKING ONTO THE MUSIC SCENE

You've got a decent voice, so why haven't you landed a record deal, become a recording artist and headlined your own cross-country concert tour? Why aren't you right there with Austin Mahone, ready to take on the music world?

Because it takes more than just good pipes to make it big.

Singer Joey McIntyre says no recording artist can be successful unless he or she breaks a few rules along the way.

"As a member of the New Kids on the Block, I helped sell 75 million records," he told the *Boston Herald*. "When I branched out as a solo artist, at first I had to finance my own efforts, because the record companies weren't telling me what I wanted to hear. There are so many levels of bureaucracy you have to navigate through in order to achieve any level of success in the recording industry."

Photo courtesy of AP Images

Being at the top of your game is crucial and the way to get there is practice. Alicia Keys is a great example of an artist who made this rule work. She sang backup in numerous bands until she made her breakthrough with her Grammy Award-winning song "Fallin'."

"Music came before everything, everything, everything," Keys has said. "It just meant more than anything ever meant. I would risk everything for it."

Singing in the shower is great, but really practicing your craft takes more effort. Find a vocal coach, take a class, join a band, perform in an open mic night. Practice, practice, practice.

Whatever you do, don't give up. If you keep hearing "No," find out why. Do you need a hook that sets you apart from all the other acts trying to make it big? Do you need to change your look? Is your voice better suited to a different genre? Listen to feedback, weigh your options and be persistent.

"Often, what it takes to get your demo tape listened to comes down to who you know in the industry," says Denise George, National Director Pop Promotion at Jive Records. "This is a tough industry to succeed in," George said. "You have to really want to achieve success and be willing to dedicate your life to achieving it. Britney Spears, for example, has been performing since she was in preschool."

New Kids on the Block Joey McIntyre, Danny Wood, Jordan Knight and Jonathan Knight attend a publicity event in April 2013.

Learn as much as you can about the recording industry. Read publications like *Billboard* and *Radio and Records*, so you can stay on top of music trends. Attend local shows and talk to performers between sets, many – especially those just starting out – will be willing to share tips and information.

Don't forget that many of today's hottest musicians – including Austin, Justin Bieber and Cody Simpson – were discovered thanks to the Internet. Once your sound is refined, start uploading videos. Don't know how? Ask a friend, take a class or follow online tutorials – it's really not that hard.

While it may not be any great surprise that young people use YouTube to find and/or listen to music, there's now research to back that up. According to a Nielsen Music 360 report released in August 2012, 64 percent of teens say they listen to music through YouTube. The Web's leading video-sharing site topped all other music sources cited by teens; 56 percent said they listen to music on the radio, 53 percent rely on iTunes and 50 percent listen to CDs.

No doubt, the Internet can serve as an amazing promotional tool to help new artists get discovered. Remember that you want your videos to go viral because people are amazed by your talent – not because they're laughing at your not-so-hot dance moves.

Practice, persist and get smart about the industry – your future stardom depends on it.

CHAPTER TWO
MAKING MUSIC

Austin performs at at California's Great America in August 2012.

For some it's flowers or candy or a romantic dinner for two.

Austin Mahone, however, did something a little different on Valentine's Day 2012: he released his first single, "11:11," on iTunes. The song, a pop gem inspired by the mystical powers of the time 11:11, charted at No. 19 on the Billboard Heatseekers Songs chart. It was an auspicious beginning to a promising musical career.

Three months later, on June 5, 2012, Austin released a second single called "Say Somethin'." The video for that catchy guitar-pop track capitalizes on Austin's wholesome good looks and nearly perfect smile and tells the story of trying to connect with a high school crush. It's a scenario – and song – that resonated with fans. The single charted at No. 34 on the Billboard Pop Songs chart. Within eight months of its release, the song's

Austin and his crew perform at Y100's Pre-Show at Jingle Ball Village in Fort Lauderdale in December 2012.

AUSTIN'S BTR CONNECTION

Mahomies know that Austin Mahone is a fan of Big Time Rush, so it really shouldn't have come as much of a surprise when MTV News announced the entertainers were teaming up for a TV project.

Big Time Rush announced that Austin is one of a handful of stars who will appear on the final episode of season four of their self-titled Nickelodeon series. Actor and rapper Nick Cannon, American pop duo Karmin and singer/songwriter Alexa Vega also are slated to appear in the episode, billed as "Big Time Awards Show."

The show's storyline revolves around the fictitious Tween Choice Awards, where the boy band is nominated and booked to close the show. But, before the foursome can take the stage, they uncover an evil plot to brainwash everyone in the audience. Big Time Rush must take down the bad guys and make sure the show rolls on as scheduled.

Big Time Rush airs on Nickelodeon. The show's fourth season will follow the band as they record their third album and prepare for a world tour in a changing pop-music landscape.

Kendall Schmidt, James Maslow, Carlos Pena, Jr. and Logan Henderson of Big Time Rush in Hollywood in April 2013.

> *Still without a label and with only two singles on iTunes, Austin accomplished another remarkable feat in June 2012. He sold out the 2,000-seat Best Buy Theatre in New York City in just 30 minutes.*

music video had accumulated more than 18.5 million views, proving Austin is a true force to be reckoned with on the pop scene.

"That feels amazing to know that I've come such a long way. I am so blessed to have so many amazing fans around me that have helped me reach my dreams," he told *Broken Records* magazine.

Still without a label and with only two singles on iTunes, Austin accomplished another remarkable feat in June 2012. He sold out the 2,000-seat Best Buy

Theatre in New York City in just 30 minutes. Even Austin was astonished by news of the sell-out.

"I wasn't ready for that one," he told *J-14* magazine. "I was in IHOP and when my mom told me I was like, 'Wow, that's crazy!'"

That New York City show, combined with fans clamoring for more, led Austin to take his show on the road, with performances in cities including Philadelphia, Los Angeles and Chicago.

On Dec. 3, 2012, Austin released "Say You're Just a Friend." The single, released on iTunes via Chase Records, features Flo Rida on rap vocals. The tune's catchy melody and chorus were inspired by rapper Biz Markie's 1989 song "Just a Friend."

"The single's about basically having that one person that you like very much and you have a crush on them and you tell them that you like that person more than a friend and she's saying, 'Ah, no, I like you just as friends,'" Austin told Entertainmentwise.com in April 2013. "So, I think everybody can relate to that."

Austin had long been a fan of Flo Rida, who is known for hit songs including

DUET PARTNER: ALYSSA SHOUSE

Sweater-wearing Austin Mahone sings his heart out on his cover of "No Air" (Chris Brown and Jordin Sparks). His angst-filled vocals are strong and he's handsome as ever – but who in the world is his equally fretful duet partner?

Ah, it's none other than Alyssa Shouse.

Shouse has grown up singing in school talent shows and competitions around her hometown of Ellicott City, Md. In December 2008, she began posting videos of her performances – a combination of covers and original songs – on YouTube.

"I had a lot of favorite singers on YouTube and it really made me want to do it too," she said in a 2010 interview with the online publication *YHP*. "I wanted to do it because I loved singing for people, so on YouTube I could sing for as many people as I could get. It wasn't really a way to get found, it was just a way to showcase what I love doing."

Oh, but she did "get found."

American singer/songwriter/producer/actor Jason Derulo saw Shouse's videos online and signed her to his new label, Future History, in summer 2010.

From there, she recorded and released her first single, "Overnight Celebrity." She's performed around the country and made appearances on shows including MTV's *The Seven*. As of April 2013, her YouTube channel had

Jordin Sparks and Chris Brown made "No Air" famous, but Austin and Alyssa performed a pretty decent cover of the song.

attracted 137,400 subscribers and her videos had been viewed nearly 11 million times.

Shouse says working with Derulo is as much fun as it is work. "We joke around all the time. He makes me really comfortable and we have the best time hanging out," she told Just Jared Jr. in 2011.

Derulo continues to be impressed with his online discovery. "If I had to compare her to anyone, I would say Christina Aguilera," he says. "She has a big voice in a little body."

Austin posted his duet with Shouse on YouTube in April 2012; within its first year online, the video had attracted nearly 2.6 million views.

AWARD NOMINATIONS - ALREADY!

Austin Mahone has barely dipped his toes into the entertainment industry, but he's already making an Olympian-like splash.

For starters, Austin beat out Ryan Beatty, IM5, Cimbrelli and Christina Grimmie to be named Best Breakout Star at the 2013 Radio Disney Awards.

"Wow, I've never won an award before," he said while accepting his statuette. He went on to thank his fans and his mom, "This is amazing. First of all, I want to thank all the Mahomies out there."

He was nominated for four additional awards that night: Best Male Artist, Fiercest Fans, Best Crush Song and Best Acoustic Performance. Sure, Justin Bieber won Best Male Artist, but just being nominated alongside him, Cody Simpson and Bruno Mars made Mahone a pretty happy guy.

In early 2013, Austin was nominated for a Popdust/Popstar of Tomorrow award. He was edged out by Fifth Harmony, an American five-piece girl group that was formed for the second season of *The X Factor*.

And, while he may not have gotten a trophy to go with the title, Austin was named *J-14*'s Icon of Tomorrow in late 2012. The magazine recognized "iconic" figures in 26 categories including Iconic

Song, Iconic Trendsetter, Iconic Tweeter and Iconic Couple. The 2011 winners of the Icon of Tomorrow Award have gone on to some pretty big things ... you may have heard of them ... One Direction?

It's nearly certain that Austin's mantel will be filled with awards in no time at all ... let the nominations begin.

Austin proudly accepts his Golden Mickey Mouse statuette during the 2013 Radio Disney Music Awards in Los Angeles. Photo courtesy of AP Images

"More handsome than Bieber. Yeaay."

"I LUV that song. I heard it already like 500 times I just can't get enough plus he's so cute."

"Ahhhh, I found my new favorite song – I love u Austin."

"I listen to this every time I am sad or happy. P.S. – There's no one hotter than you Austin Mahone and you are my fav singer. You're better than Pink, JB, Drake and Hollywood Undead combined."

Within just two months of its release, the video for "Heart in My Hand" had attracted more than 2.8 million views – a sure sign that fans are clamoring for more.

Even as celebrity status sets in, Austin remains devoted to his music and his fans.

His days are jam-packed with radio interviews, TV appearances, magazine interviews and concerts. A May 2013 show in Mexico City offered proof that Austin's fame reaches far beyond the U.S. borders. Hundreds of Mahomies waited for him outside Universal Republic's Mexico City offices and they went absolutely gaga when they finally caught a glimpse of their idol. Members of the mostly female crowd screamed and squealed when Austin waved from a second floor window – some girls even climbed trees to get closer to the singer.

Undeterred by all the distractions, Austin is putting the finishing touches on his full-length debut album. The project, which will feature production from Bei Maejor, will be marketed and distributed by Chase/Universal Republic.

"I'm getting pressure from my fans and I'm still working on it, but the sound is going to be like 'Say Somethin' – happy, upbeat," Austin told *Bop/Tiger Beat*. "I'm also going to have some ballads on there, maybe a couple urban songs, more R&B. But it's basically going to be mostly like 'Say Somethin'."

Alright, say Mahomies, just bring it on. ★

Austin and T-Pain pose backstage at Power 96.1's Jingle Ball 2012 in December 2012 in Atlanta.

AUSTIN'S MUSICAL INFLUENCES

Artists develop their own sound based on the influences in their lives.

They often reinterpret music from their childhoods, add recycled rhythms from their teen years and create arrangements that are both inspired by the past, yet are still oh, so very original. Everyone does it.

• Michael Jackson said he was influenced by artists including Little Richard, James Brown and Diana Ross.

• Beyonce Knowles said Mariah Carey's singing influenced her to practice vocal runs as a child.

• Michael Jackson, Stevie Wonder, Usher and Justin Timberlake are among Justin Bieber's many musical influences.

Austin Mahone is no different. His music is made up of a little bit of everything.

"I grew up listening to country music because that was what my mom listened to at the time," he said in a March 2013 interview for VEVO LIFT. He enjoyed singing along to George Strait and the first concert he ever attended was headlined by country star Kenny Chesney.

As he matured and began branching out musically, Austin began to listen to other genres including R&B and pop. He became a fan of artists as diverse as rappers Flo Rida and Drake, R&B artist Ne-Yo, pop singer Justin Bieber, and country/pop artist Taylor Swift.

"I found an artist named T-Pain so I really attached to his music and loved it so much," he said. "That's what really crossed me over from listening to country."

Singling out the performer whose style has been most influential to his career is difficult for Austin, but he finally settles on an answer – Chris Brown.

"An inspiration to me would have to be Chris Brown because he's an amazing singer, an amazing dancer, he's an awesome performer," he said, noting that his favorite Chris Brown song is "Don't Judge Me."

"(I like) the lyrics behind it and I also like how the song was made – you know, the production of it," he said.

Is a future collaboration with some of his musical idols a possibility? Austin certainly wouldn't rule it out.

"I think an awesome Mahone, T-Pain, Chris Brown song would be pretty cool," he said.

> *"I think an awesome Mahone, T-Pain, Chris Brown song would be pretty cool," Austin said.*

OPENING FOR TAYLOR SWIFT

When Austin Mahone got the call that he would be opening for selected shows of Taylor Swift's highly anticipated RED Tour, he was elated.

"I still can't believe I'm opening for Taylor! I'm so appreciative and excited for this opportunity," he told Artist Direct. "Getting to play in stadiums, and it's with one of the biggest artists in the world! I can't wait!"

Prior to the tour's kick off, Austin told Just Jared Jr. he was thrilled with the idea of being able to perform for such huge audiences; several of the stadium shows will have crowds of 70,000 or more.

"I've never performed for that big of a crowd before," he said. "I'm not really sure what to expect because I've never been on tour before, but I think it's going to be fun. I've been rehearsing for a while now, just getting ready for all the shows."

Austin admits he's long been a fan of Taylor Swift. He was actually starstruck when, in early 2012, he got to meet her in a Nashville café.

"She walked in and I went up to her and was like, 'Can I have a picture with you?' I got a picture of her and I told her that I'm on YouTube and I sing. She was like, 'That's really cool. Keep up the hard work. Never give up on your dreams.' It's crazy. Now a year later, I'm going on tour with her."

Austin took another photo of himself with Taylor a year later – this time backstage prior to their show in Detroit, Mich. He posted the picture on Instagram with the caption: "It's been a year, but we've finally re-united! Thanks again @TaylorSwift13 for having me on the tour!! #REDTOUR"

Austin's shows with Taylor Swift were scheduled throughout the spring and summer of 2013 and were not consecutive:

May 4	Ford Field, Detroit, Mich.
May 25	Dallas Cowboys Stadium, Arlington, Texas
June 14	Rogers Centre, Toronto, Canada
June 15	Rogers Centre, Toronto, Canada
June 22	Investors Group Field, Winnipeg, Canada
June 29	BC Place, Vancouver, Canada
July 6	Heinz Field, Pittsburgh, Penn.
July 13	MetLife Stadium, East Rutherford, N.J.
July 19	Lincoln Financial Field, Philadelphia, Penn.
July 20	Lincoln Financial Field, Philadelphia, Penn.
July 26	Gillette Stadium, Foxboro, Mass.
July 27	Gillette Stadium, Foxboro, Mass.
Aug. 10	Soldier Field, Chicago, Ill.

Austin, Taylor Swift and Ed Sheeran gather in Club Red prior to their May 4, 2013, show at Ford Field in Detroit; it was the first of 13 North American dates that Austin appeared as part of the RED Tour.

CHAPTER THREE

HEIR TO THE POP THRONE?

The comparisons were inevitable.

• Justin Bieber was discovered thanks to YouTube. Austin Mahone was discovered thanks to YouTube.

• Justin connects with fans via Twitter and Skype. Austin connects with fans via Twitter and Skype.

• Pop star Justin is known for his hair, his stylish sneakers and his dance moves. Pop star Austin is known for his hair, his stylish sneakers and his dance moves.

• JB was raised by a single mother. AM was raised by a single mother.

The Hollywood Reporter has referred to Austin as "Baby Bieber." *The Daily Mail* has called him the "New Justin Bieber." AOL.com has referred to the Texas native as "the second coming of Bieber." Yahoo News went so far as to ask: "Justin Bieber vs. Austin Mahone: Are They The Same Person?"

Even the *Wall Street Journal* got into the act when, in October 2012, columnist Marshall Heyman wrote: "Today's youth don't dream about playing center field for the Yankees or piloting a spacecraft to Mars. Instead, they aspire to become the next Bieber." Heyman's article went on to name Austin as one of the five leading contenders to be the next Justin Bieber.

Austin says the comparisons to Bieber are flattering and bring with them a certain amount of pressure. JB was, after all, named by *Forbes* as the third most powerful celeb in the world in 2012.

"I hope to be as successful as him someday, but I just want people to give me a chance, see me as my own artist and as Austin. That's all I ask," he told *Extra* in April 2013.

Austin's fans, however, are often annoyed by all the talk of Justin.

"People say that Austin is the new Justin Bieber – I don't think that at all," fan

The Making of Mahomies

Everybody knows that Austin Mahone's fans are Mahomies. It's a name he came up with himself.

"I was sitting in my room with my best friend and we were talking about all these crazy fan names that people have and so we were like, 'If we had a fan base one day what would we name them?' And I came up with Mahomies for mine and I guess I told someone and word kind of spread," he told *4 Music*.

Austin and Justin Bieber strike a pose while visiting the Elvis Duran Z100 Morning Show in New York City in June 2012.

AUSTIN VS. JUSTIN

How about a side-by-side comparison of these two totally ahhhh-some performers?

	AUSTIN	JUSTIN
Middle name	Carter	Drew
Rightie or leftie?	Rightie	Leftie
Eye color	Hazel	Brown
Instruments	Piano, guitar, drums	Trumpet, guitar, piano, drums
Fans called	Mahomies	Beliebers
Sport of choice	Basketball, football	Ice hockey
Favorite team	San Antonio Spurs	Cleveland Cavaliers, Toronto Maple Leafs
Astrological sign	Aries	Pisces
National anthem	*Star Spangled Banner*	*O Canada*
Twitter followers	2.7 million	39.4 million
Favorite color	Red	Purple
Musical influences	Drake, Justin Bieber, Ne-Yo	Michael Jackson, Usher
Favorite foods	Pizza, Ziti, Lasagna, Chicken Alfredo	Spaghetti Bolognese
Favorite ice cream flavor	Vanilla, Chocolate	Cotton Candy
Favorite candy	Hershey's Kisses	Marshmallow Peeps
Personal motto	"Make the most of every opportunity, because you only get one chance."	"Family first."

AUSTIN

JUSTIN

Austin attends the 7th Annual J-14 magazine InTune Concert in New York City in September 2012.

Maggie Benzenhafer told MTV News as she waited outside his show at New York's Best Buy Theatre in June 2012. "I think Austin's going to be the new Austin Mahone."

That Austin's accomplishments are being compared to Bieber's shouldn't really surprise – or irritate anyone. After all, comparisons like this have been going on for years.

Lady Gaga has been hailed as "the new Madonna."

Bruno Mars has been called "the reincarnation of Michael Jackson."

The band fun. has been described as "this generation's Queen."

Jennifer Hudson has been described as "the new Whitney Houston."

Most of these assessments come about quite naturally. You hear a song

Austin doesn't mind comparisons to Justin Bieber – they are both great singers and dancers – but he'd like to be judged on his own merits.

IT'S ALL ABOUT THE HAIR

Yes, Austin Mahone's smile is adorable and his vocals are velvety, but everybody knows pop stardom is about having the right hair. Good news – Austin's locks are tops.

In September 2012, Austin got a trim and tweeted a photo of his new, shorter 'do along with the caption: "What do you think? New hairstyle? :)"

MTV's Buzzworth Blog writers immediately responded: "We really appreciate that Austin asked us for our opinion, and we're gonna be completely honest about the way we feel: WE. ADORE. IT! Not only is the hair-to-gel ratio absolutely perfect (dudes, crunchy hair is just NOT OK – capiche?!)"

It wasn't the first time Austin sent his fans into a hair-induced frenzy – and it won't be the last.

On June 6, 2012, Austin tweeted a Photoshopped picture of himself with poorly dyed golden locks, accompanied by the message: "What do you guys think of my new dyed hair? (: "

Later the same day, he sent out photographic proof that his brunette hair was still very brunette along with this message: "Hahaha I'm just playin! (; I would never dye my hair that drastic!"

On March 29, 2013, Austin tweeted to fans that he was going to get a haircut. A follow-up tweet read: "AHHHHH she messed up my hair!!! WE HAD TO SHAVE IT!!" He eventually revealed that he was only joking and sent out a photo of his new hairstyle (which looked a lot like an old Justin Bieber hairstyle).

With all this fuss about follicles, it's interesting to note that Austin wears a hat almost everywhere he goes.

"The reason behind that is because I hate the way my hair looks," he told Just Jared Jr. in February 2013, "so I wear a hat to cover it up."

Girls love Austin's locks, but he'd prefer to hide them under a hat.

by a new artist, you try to describe that artist's style and sound to a friend and, in doing so, you rely on descriptions of music your friend already knows, such as "She sounds a little like Adele." Your friend knows exactly what Adele sounds like, so she can begin to imagine this new artist's contralto. Similar comparisons can be made for appearance, style or background. Before you know it, the media is suggesting the same sort of similarities.

These evaluations and labels don't suggest an artist is an imitator (though many openly admit to having shaped their style on the riffs of those who came before them). Instead, they often make the "new" artist more relatable for music fans and actually encourage people to sample music they might otherwise never hear.

Yes, Austin does admire the success Bieber has enjoyed. Yes, he understands that they were discovered in similar ways and attract the same sort of young, mostly female audiences. Still, he promises he won't be emulating any of JB's most recent bad boy behavior. A few of Bieber's headline-grabbing discretions?

• Posting a cartoon of himself naked in bed with a "Belieber."

• Disrobing in a Polish airport.

• Being accused of battery by a neighbor.

• Having narcotics discovered during a search of his tour bus.

• Having his monkey seized by customs officials in Germany.

• Scuffling with the paparazzi.

The Globe and Mail, a newspaper published in his native Canada, has labeled Bieber "a national embarrassment." *Forbes* magazine has referred to him as a "spoiled brat" and the *Business Insider* has run articles about his "downward spiral."

What About Alex?

Austin Mahone famously posted those first YouTube videos with his best bud, Alex Constancio. What happened to Alex when Austin got famous?

Good news, the guys are still best friends. Alex doesn't sing much (though he does enjoy lip synching). He often travels with Austin, acts (he was in Rebecca Black's "Person of Interest" video), has his own merchandise line, and he's amassed nearly 335,000 followers on Twitter.

HE'S FASHIONABLE —FROM HEAD TO TOE

Austin Mahone is a fashion trendsetter. The handsome brunette is known for wearing baseball caps – typically backward. And, like any self-respecting pop star, he loves his outrageously stylish tennis shoes.

"I think I have more hats only because I have a hat for pretty much every day of the year," he told radio interviewer Mike Adam in early 2013. "I mean, I've always loved hats and sneakers, but once I started getting more into the music and doing a lot more photo shoots, they just sort of started flooding in."

Even still, Austin's shoe collection is impressive – so impressive, in fact, that VEVO

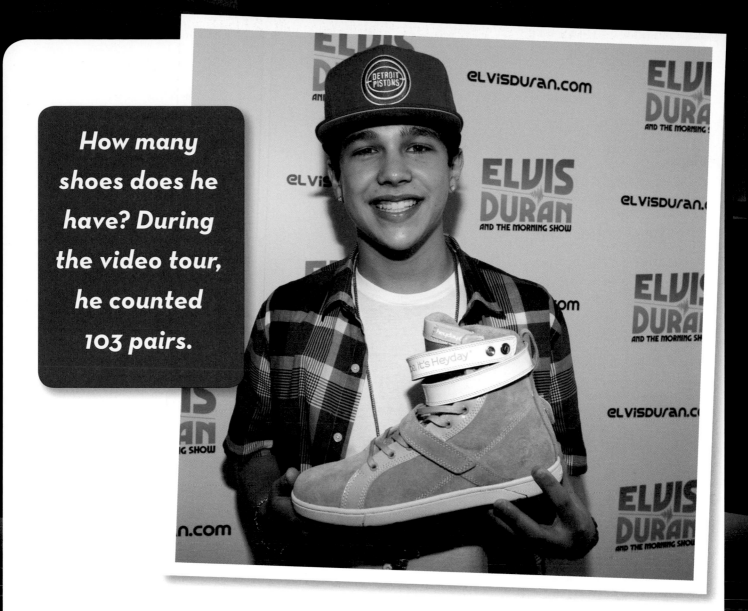

LIFI posted a video tour of his closet in March 2013. The three-minute segment has been viewed more than 350,000 times.

During the tour, Austin shows off the first sneakers from his extensive collection: a pair of white and red Nike Dunks. He then points to a spot in his impeccable closet (does it always look that neat?) where he keeps his favorite shoes. Among his top picks? A pair of all-red Puma high tops, some white Adidas, blue Nike Dunks and a pair of tan Timberland hiking boots that "go with anything."

Sure, most of the shoes are purely for fashion and he loves color coordinating with outfits, but Austin says some shoes actually help him dance better.

Austin admits that Nike and Adidas are his favorite brands, but adds, "If I see a pair of shoes that I like, then I'll just snatch them up."

How many shoes does he have? During the video tour, he counted 103 pairs.

"I was hoping I would break 100, so I think I met my goal," he said, noting that he's had as many as 105 pairs – but he lost two in a basketball bet with friends.

"People say that Austin is the new Justin Bieber – I don't think that at all," fan Maggie Benzenhafer told MTV News. *"I think Austin's going to be the new Austin Mahone."*

All a-Twitter

Austin Mahone loves online social networking. He especially loves connecting with his fans through Twitter. As of May 2013, he had 2.7 million Twitter followers and was gaining new followers at a rate of 6,820 per day.

Austin's tweets are rarely earth-shattering. Rather, he tends to update fans about what he's doing or where he is; he might tell a joke or make a random observation. On average, Austin tweets eight times each day. Some samples:

May 9, 2013: Dance rehearsals!!!

May 6, 2013: I need a button on my phone that will let me erase messages on other peoples phones that I've sent and regret very shortly after. lol

April 30, 2013: It's so funny trying to talk to people with the little Spanish I know!

April 26, 2013: I CAN'T WAIT FOR THE RADIO DISNEY AWARDS TOMORROW!!! #firstperformer

Austin says seeing the negative attention heaped on Bieber has made him more determined than ever to stay on the straight-and-narrow.

"I definitely have my family and my friends to keep me grounded and stay humble and I just gotta enjoy everything while I'm here and just enjoy life. It might not be there forever," he told EntertainmentWise.

For those who are wondering, Austin did get a chance to meet Mr. Bieber in early 2012 (prior to most of JB's most notorious foul-ups) when the two entertainers were being interviewed at the same radio station.

"I was in the elevator and I went up to the floor and I got out of the elevator and he was standing right there, just like chilling. I said 'What's up Justin?' and I gave him a high-five and then he went to his interview. I went to mine and then we got some pictures and it was cool."

That first encounter didn't give the two pop stars much time to chat, but the Biebs was kind enough to offer Austin advice over the radio.

"He said that no matter how big or successful I get, not to stop and be like 'Oh, I'm here,'" Austin recounted for *Access Hollywood*. "He said to keep going and do different things and to keep pushing and just keep going to the top."

The top? Yes, that's exactly where Austin is headed. ★

RISING STARS IN THE POST-JB ERA

Austin Mahone is definitely making waves in the music industry, but he's not alone. These five artists are among rising pop stars you'll want to give a listen to:

MAX SCHNEIDER

A Manhattan native, Max has worked as an actor (*Law & Order*, *How to Rock*) and model (he posed with Madonna for a Dolce & Gabbana ad campaign).

Max is a talented singer/songwriter. His song "Last One Standing" was featured on *How To Rock* and his song "Show You How To Do" was featured on the show *Shake It Up*. Max asked his fans to help him fund his upcoming album *Nothing Without Love* and, thanks to Kickstarter, he was able to pay for it. The first single from the new CD was released in May 2013.

CONOR MAYNARD

R&B artist Ne-Yo reached out to Conor after he saw his cover of "Beautiful Monster" on YouTube. The two began communicating via Skype, which led to a recording contract with the EMI subsidiary Parlophone.

In January 2012, it was announced that Conor won MTV's Brand New for 2012 award. His first album, *Contrast*, featuring songs written with Frank Ocean and Pharrell Williams, debuted in August 2012 at No. 1 in the United Kingdom.

CONOR

MAX

CODY SIMPSON

This Australian-born singer got his start – surprise! – by posting videos of his performances on YouTube. He was subsequently discovered by Grammy-nominated record producer Shawn Campbell.

Cody is currently signed to Atlantic Records. His debut album, *Paradise*, was released on Sept. 28, 2012; a four-song teaser EP, *Preview to Paradise*, was released on June 12, 2012.

CODY

JENNIFER CHUNG

Not all Justin Bieber-wannabes are guys – Jennifer is proof of that.

MTV Iggy writers love this Korean-American artist. Her YouTube channel JenniferJChung has more than 138,000 subscribers, and the video of her singing Alicia Keys' "No One" has more than 5.6 million views. As of now unsigned, MTV predicts: "This soothing voice and fun personality will one day take her to the top."

GREYSON CHANCE

Greyson's 2010 performance at a school festival was taped and posted on YouTube, where it became a gigantic hit – with more than 50.6 million views as of May 2013.

After seeing Greyson's video, Ellen DeGeneres invited him to perform on her show. This first performance was followed by a second appearance, during which DeGeneres announced Greyson would be the first artist signed to her recording label eleveneleven. His debut album, *Hold On 'Til the Night*, was released in August 2011.

JENNIFER

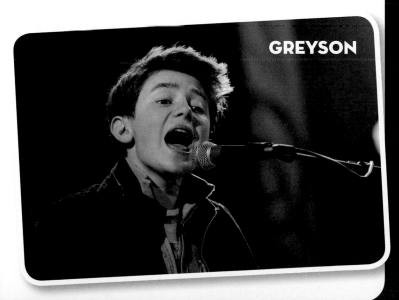

GREYSON

CHAPTER FOUR
ARE YOU A MAHOMIE?

New Jersey teen Ashley Filipe got to see Austin Mahone perform at New York's Highline Ballroom in March 13, as part of MTV's Artists to Watch showcase. The sold-out crowd chanted his name and sang along to his hit single "Say Somethin'," while Austin reached out to greet fans near the stage.

The whole scene made Filipe a little woozy – in a good way. "He touched my hand five times," she told *MTV News*. "I was going to pass out. To be honest, I was shaking."

Fellow concert-goer Megan McHale, had a similar, stomach-churning reaction when Austin grabbed her cell phone during his performance and snapped a selfie.

"I want to throw up, I'm so excited," McHale screamed. "I'm speechless."

It seems Austin Mahone has the kind of star power that makes girls' stomachs churn and knees go weak. That dazzling smile, that beautiful, thick hair, those

> *The sold-out crowd chanted his name and sang along to his hit single "Say Somethin'," while Austin reached out to greet fans near the stage.*

high-energy dance moves – AM's got the stuff that has fans blogging and vlogging and Tweeting at breakneck speed. The really great part is that he knows he wouldn't be where he is at now without those fans, so he remains devoted to interacting with them.

Austin, after all, got his start posting videos on YouTube. Positive feedback encouraged him to post more videos. He blogged. He tweeted. He video

chatted with fans. Austin says all that direct interaction has both propelled his career and helped him develop a strong relationship with his fans. He's offered video tours of his closet and bedroom (which is decorated with posters made by his fans). He's uploaded videotaped pool matches with his mother and basketball games with his pals. And, he's shared videos of his first driving lessons.

Austin blows kisses to the crowd during a December 2012 show in Atlanta.

ALL A-TWITTER

Austin Mahone loves to stay connected with his fans and one of his favorite ways to do that is through Twitter. As of May 2013, the Texas native had more than 2.7 million followers and was gaining new Twitter followers at a rate of almost 6,500 per day.

Using 140 characters or less, Austin lets fans know what he's doing, where he's at, what he's eating, what he's thinking and so on. Fans love it and frequently re-tweet Austin's messages – spreading the word about his music, award nominations and TV appearances. Of course, Twitter is a two-way street; Austin follows nearly 20,000 people, many of them fans.

Here's a sampling of some of Austin's micro-blogging:

@AustinMahone: The best feeling is when I look over at you and you are already looking at me. *May 12, 2013*

@AustinMahone: Happy Mother's Day to the #1 Mom in the world! @MicheleMahone U mean everything to me – I love you with all my heart. Hope ur day is amazing. *May 12, 2013*

@AustinMahone: It's funny how you can do nice things for people all the time and they never notice, but once you make one mistake it's never forgotten. *May 9, 2013*

@AustinMahone: The best kind of kiss is when you have to stop because you can't help but smile. *May 8, 2013*

@AustinMahone: Mom's spaghetti hits the spot! *May 8, 2013*

@AustinMahone: I need a button on my phone that will let me erase messages on other people's phones that I've sent and regret very shortly after. lol. *May 6, 2013*

@AustinMahone: WHAT AN AMAZING FIRST SHOW!!! :D Thank u again @TaylorSwift13 #REDTOUR. *May 4, 2013*

@AustinMahone: Just got a nice warm welcome at the airport from the Mexican Mahomies! *April 29, 2013*

@AustinMahone: My room feels like Antarctica!! *April 25, 2013*

@AustinMahone: I think I'm gonna go to Walmart and buy a 6-pack of Crush! haha it's still weird to me that my face is on a can of soda! *April 23, 2013*

@AustinMahone: They told me I wouldn't shine, that my dreams were stones of gray. But look at me now, living life. *April 19, 2013*

@AustinMahone: Watching the hunger games... "Welcome to the 74th annual Hunger Games!" Me: Ohhhhhh my gaaawd! How. Does. This. Happen. *April 14, 2013*

@AustinMahone: I am quite certain that with a nice guitar and a recording contract, I could save the world. *April 11, 2013*

@AustinMahone: BEST BIRTHDAY EVER! Thank you guys so much for your awesome tweets and birthday videos! – I LOVE YOU SO MUCH!!!!! *April 4, 2013*

@AustinMahone: Ballin at the White House on Obama's court! #EasterEggRoll @AttheWH. *March 31, 2013*

@AustinMahone: Be yourself. Be proud of who you are, and don't let anyone change that. We're all freaks. No one on earth is the same. *March 27, 2013*

"I try to keep it as real as possible," Austin told Fuse TV, "so they can see me how I am, in my environment, in my room, stuff like that."

Even while he was doing his own marketing and scheduling, Austin was surprised by his own fame when, in October 2011, he tweeted to fans in Chicago that he was planning a simple meet-and-greet in Millennium Park. Thousands of Mahomies rushed to the area causing quite an influx of excited and hyperventilating tweens and teens. Police whisked Austin and his mother away to a secure building next to the park until they could figure out what to do. Austin eventually took to Twitter to let fans know the event had been cancelled: *Mahomies, it's really hard for me to say this but i can't do a meetup on*

Famous Fan

One of Austin Mahone's most famous fans also happens to be Justin Bieber's ex Selena Gomez. Call it Lone Star love, Gomez grew up in Grand Prairie Texas, about 250 miles from Austin's hometown of San Antonio.

this trip – the police won't let me do it, I'm so sorry ... Don't worry I'm okay and you didn't do anything wrong!!

"It was really weird because I didn't have any security with me – it was just me and my mom – and I thought I was going to go and meet like 10 girls and I went there and it was like 1,000 girls and the police shut the whole thing down," he told *Access Hollywood*. "It was just crazy, just girls coming from all directions at me. It was just a whole new experience for me – coming from a super small town doing nothing and going to Chicago and getting destroyed by girls."

That fanatic fan gathering signaled to Austin that he needed a management team and he needed security. Both have since been put in place and subsequent fan encounters have been substantially less frightening.

Backup Plan

If music doesn't work out, Austin Mahone has another career path he wouldn't mind following – basketball. He used to play point guard when he was in school.

HOW TO BE A FANTASTIC FAN

Some musicians' fans are just plain rude. Austin Mahone is proud to say his fans are a pretty respectful – and energetic – group. Anyone can say they're a Mahomie, but adhering to these five guidelines will ensure Austin's fans remain the best in the business:

1. Know Your Stuff. Read magazine and newspaper interviews, watch Austin's TV appearances, follow him on Twitter and, of course, listen to his music. Get your Austin info from a variety of sources so you can promptly spot misinformation.

2. Don't Stalk. Speak positively about Austin, support him and his music, but also remember to respect his privacy – that also goes for his family, friends and girlfriends. R-E-S-P-E-C-T.

3. Don't Dis. While we're talking about respect, we might as well mention respecting other artists, fans and fandoms. You've chosen to support an artist you deem worthy of your time and attention; others have chosen to support other musicians that suit their own tastes and preferences. Austin is a terrific musician – but he's not the only musician. Don't dis non-Mahomies.

4. Be Reasonable. It's okay to tell a friend why you don't care for another celebrity, but do it without getting too personal. No bashing and no bullying. Don't sabotage other celebrities' appearances or other fandoms' votes or meetings. Disruption is not reasonable.

5. Don't Go Crazy. Yes, it's understandable that you'd be excited if you got a chance to meet Austin – but imagine the noise and stress to which he's constantly being exposed. Showing your love doesn't have to mean screaming nonstop during a 30-minute set. And, no matter the circumstances: safety comes first. Don't push, don't climb fences or open doors you don't have permission to open, don't break traffic rules. Be smart!

Photo courtesy of AP Images

Fans cheer on Austin as he performs at the San Jose, Calif., State Event Center in December 2012.

With throngs of fans growing, Austin still graciously stops for photos, to shake hands and, when it's possible, to autograph memorabilia. He continues his Twitter conversations with Mahomies; in addition to his 2.7 million followers, he follows more than 20,000 people – many of them his own fans.

And, the young Texas native is coming to grips with the fact that his fame has reached beyond U.S. borders.

Even before his debut album was released, Austin had amassed a legion of fans from around the world. He made stops in England in late 2012 and in Germany in early 2013. Meanwhile, fans in countries ranging from Japan and Australia to Scotland and Costa Rica had begun petitions aimed at getting Austin to perform there.

In May 2013, Austin was swarmed by fans when he traveled to Mexico City.

Austin answers questions for Canadian fans during an interview at MuchMusic Headquarters in Toronto in December 2012.

Hundreds of Mahomies waited for him outside Universal Republic offices and they went absolutely berserk when they finally caught a glimpse of their idol. Video clips posted by Austin's record company showed the largely female crowd screaming uncontrollably when the pop star appeared at a second floor window. The girls jumped, screamed, chanted and even climbed trees to get a better view of the singer. For his part, a sombrero-wearing Austin giggled, waved and videotaped some of the madness on his cell phone.

Longtime fans are realistic. Sure, they were cheering him on when no

Three Fun Facts

Think you know everything there is to know about Austin Mahone?

Did you know:

1. He considers himself a paranoid person.
2. He hates slow drivers.
3. He's obsessed with pizza and eats it nearly every day.

Are You Austin's Dream Girl?

Sincerity. That's what Austin Mahone told *Popstar* magazine he looks for in a potential girlfriend. First date turn-offs? "No manners, on her phone."

"I like a girl who wants me for who I am," Austin said in a video interview for a fan site. "I like a nice smile and nice eyes."

one else even knew his name, but they understand that Austin's increasing fame will put more demands on his time and attention. Video chats from his bedroom aren't likely to be as commonplace. Catching his attention at a stadium concert won't be as easy as it was at a free mall show a couple of years ago. Things change; for Austin those changes have been massive.

During a March 2013 live chat, fans repeatedly Tweeted their love to Austin. Then, this message popped up:

@ObeyMahoneee: *I hope you still* **interact** *with your* **fans** *when you hit like 10 million followers.*

Austin was quick to respond in the exact way fans hoped he would:

@AustinMahone: *you know i will! (: ★*

AM APPAREL AND MORE

Dreaming of having Austin Mahone wrap his arms around you? We can't guarantee that's going to happen, but thanks to a wide array of available AM apparel, you can now snuggle up inside an Austin hoody.

Austin-inspired merchandise is available at his appearances and via his official website: www.austinmahone.com.

You can decorate your room with an Austin Mahone poster or pillow. Or, you can take the handsome singer to school with you in the form of an Austin bookmark or pen.

Of course, Austin's image is also emblazoned across T-shirts in more than 20 different designs and colors. There are also bracelets and hooded sweatshirts, both emblazoned with Austin's motto: "Haters gonna hate, Mahomies gonna love."

As Austin's fame grows so do his merchandising possibilities. Judging by those who've gone before him, there's no limit to the types of items on which his image might be printed. Some of the most outlandish fan merchandise out there? We're glad you asked:

• Detroit techno producer Omar S sells his own Omar S branded ice cube trays. What fan wouldn't want to be reminded of his favorite artist every time he wants a cold beverage?

• Love Justin Bieber? You can celebrate your birthday with a very unofficial JB piñata available through online party suppliers.

• The alternative rock band Weezer proudly sells Weezer-branded Snuggies via its website. Known as "Wuggies," the $30 blankets with sleeves, are available in three colors as well as a zebra-inspired print.

• In support of its single "Broken, Beat, & Scarred," heavy metal band Metallica offered up a collectible bandage tin. The $10 package, complete with band logo, contains 25 black adhesive bandages featuring the band's logo in red.

• The rock band KISS, long known for its face paint and flamboyant costumes, has had more than its share of unusual merchandise over the year. There have been caskets and cremation urns, Pez dispensers and biking shorts. Now, there are Kiss branded Mr. Potato Head dolls. The four figurines, which look like Kiss in spud form, cost $65.

Austin signs autographs as he arrives at Nickelodeon's 26th Annual Kids' Choice Awards in March 2013.

HOT SINGERS, HOT LYRICS

You love music. You love guys. And you love today's hottest male musicians. But are you really listening to the words they're singing?

Here's the test: Match these hunky singers to their lyrics. Answers are at the bottom of the page.

PITBULL

ADAM

JASON

1. **Cody Simpson**

2. **Usher**

3. **Jason Derulo**

4. **Taio Cruz**

5. **Chris Brown**

6. **Adam Levine**

7. **Austin Mahone**

8. **Pitbull**

9. **Drake**

10. **David Guetta**

11. **Bruno Mars**

12. **Justin Bieber**

A. "You know a lot of girls be...thinking my songs about them, this is not to get confused, this one's for you."

B. "Body rock, girl, I can feel your body rock. Take a bow, you're on the hottest ticket now."

C. "I want to be best. I want to be worst. I want to be the gravity in your universe."

D. "Burnin' up, burnin' up. Show 'em what you got."

E. "So dance, dance like it's the last, last night of your life, life."

F. "It's a beautiful night. We're looking for something dumb to do."

G. "I came to dance, dance, dance, dance."

H. "This melody was meant for you, just sing along to my stereo."

I. "I'm feeling like a star, you can't stop my shine. I'm lovin' cloud nine, my head's in the sky."

J. "You changed my whole life. Don't know what you're doing to me with your love."

K. "One, two, three, four. Uno, dos, tres, cuatro."

L. "I'm bulletproof, nothing to lose. Fire away, fire away. Ricochet, you take your aim."

Answers

USHER

BRUNO

CHAPTER FIVE
WHAT DOES THE FUTURE HOLD?

Austin Mahone has been touring the United States and Europe, selling out smaller venues and opening stadium shows for one of the biggest stars on the planet. He's fully devoted to his craft and he has been doing hundreds of radio shows and television appearances nationwide. He's got his own management company and a record deal estimated to be worth $3 million to $4 million.

Yes, Austin is on top of the world.

Or, he will be when his debut album is finally released in Fall 2013. He's already released a string of catchy, danceable pop songs, but the album – originally slated for a April 2013 drop date – has been a little slow to come together. Austin's manager Rocco Valdes says that's because pinpointing Austin's sound took longer than anticipated.

"We were getting tracks in from so many great writers and producers and it was all over the place," Valdes told *Details* magazine, mentioning established hit-makers including Max Martin (Ace of Base, Backstreet Boys, Britney Spears), RedOne (Lady Gaga, Jennifer Lopez), Steve Mac (One Direction, Kelly Clarkson, Westlife), and Savan Kotecha (Britney Spears, One Direction). "I think Austin's lane is pop. I want this album to sound like the pop I grew up on – 'N Sync, Backstreet Boys, Britney – only updated."

RedOne, who produced the Lady Gaga hits "Just Dance" and "Poker Face," has been brought in to executive produce the album and provide big-picture guidance.

"It's been a little challenging," Austin told *Details*, "but I know my fans are gonna love it."

> **He's got his own management company and a record deal estimated to be worth $3 million to $4 million.**
>
> **Yes, Austin is on top of the world.**

Austin poses backstage during a December 2012 show in Atlanta.

While he waits for that album to come out, Austin continues to do what he does best – entertain and interact. He's excited about the prospect of promoting the album around the world.

"I can't wait to meet my fans in other countries," he told the website Musichel in March 2013.

Of course, Austin knows that celebrity often comes with its detractors – sometimes in the form of paid music critics. He knows their opinions matter because they generally broadcast their thoughts to a broad audience via newspaper, magazine, radio or Internet. And he's realistic enough to understand not every critic is going to love every song.

That said, early reviews of Austin's recordings and performances have been mostly positive. A sampling:

"(Austin) Mahone delivered an impressive performance complete with choreographed dances with his backup dancers. His finale of his new single, 'Say You're Just a Friend,' was met with more screams from the adoring teens and even some parents."

—Kelsey Auman in the *Buffalo (N.Y.) News*, writing about a December 2012 show at HSBC Arena

Give That Man a Burger

On more than one occasion, Austin Mahone has given a shout out to his favorite burger chain: Whataburger. It's a reference that's left many of his fans wondering what he's talking about. Whataburger was started in 1950 in Corpus Christi, Texas, by Harmon Dobson – a man determined to serve a burger so big that it took two hands to hold, and so good that after a single bite customers couldn't help but exclaim, "What a burger!" There are now 200 Whataburgers located across the southern United States.

"Austin Mahone is about to straight up conquer pop music. That takeover has been well underway for a while, and his latest single 'Say You're Just a Friend' featuring Flo Rida proves to be the next massive step forward to the top ... With a presence of his own, an arsenal of hits already, and a whole lot of swagger, pop just might have a new king on its hands."

—Rick Florino for ArtistDirect.com, in his December 2012 review of "Say You're Just a Friend"

ARE YOU FOLLOWING AUSTIN?

Austin Mahone is a Twitter master. As of mid-May 2013, he had amassed nearly 2.7 million followers on the social networking site. It's an impressive figure for sure, but Austin is by no means the tweetingest tweeter on the planet. Twitaholic.com tracks top Twitter users based on followers. According to that website's computations, which are updated daily, the world's top Twitter users as of May 22, 2013, are:

Austin's Twitter stature is nothing to be ashamed of. In fact, the young pop star's legion of followers ranks him No. 422 among the world's 200 million Twitter users. Austin has more followers than some fairly notable folks, including: former Vice President Al Gore (425th), NBA great Kobe Bryant (No. 437th), Pope Francis (458th), actor/comedian Jamie Foxx (517th) and actress/singer Jennifer Hudson (593rd).

1. Justin Bieber (justinbieber)
    39,444,187 followers
2. Lady Gaga (ladygaga)
    37,492,181 followers
3. Katy Perry (katyperry)
    36,728,044 followers
4. Barack Obama (BarackObama)
    31,721,747 followers
5. Rihanna (rihanna)
    29,654,824 followers
6. YouTube (YouTube)
    27,947,511 followers
7. Taylor Swift (taylorswift13)
    27,636,732 followers
8. Britney Spears (britneyspears)
    27,000,434 followers
9. Shakira (shakira)
    20,728,194 followers
10. Justin Timberlake (jtimberlake)
    20,340,781 followers

Austin with the current No. 1 Twitter user, Justin Bieber.

RED Tour mates Ed Sheeran, Taylor Swift and Austin Mahone pose backstage before their sold-out show at Ford Field in Detroit.

"(Austin) Mahone skipped the live band in favor of four male dancers and a DJ. His music ('Say Somethin',' 'Hey Shawty') is standard teen-pop fluff, and he's clearly modeled after Justin Bieber. But Mahone, 16, is a confident, capable and charming performer ... Mahone wasn't always on key, but it's almost impossible not to be swayed by his earnestness."

—Joey Guerra in the *Houston Chronicle*, writing about a March 2013 show at RodeoHouston

"Mahone did not disappoint, igniting deafening screams when he hit the

For Austin, sneakers are the perfect red carpet footwear. He wore these high-tops to the 2013 Billboard Music Awards.

Radio personality Elvis Duran and Austin attend the Y100 Jingle Ball in Fort Lauderdale in December 2012.

Austin performs during the 2013 Radio Disney Music Awards in April 2013.

stage and opened with 'Say Somethin'.' Backed by four dancers, a DJ/MC and occasionally a couple of backup singers, he showed off a dance-oriented, hip-hop/pop sound. He's more confident than the guy on the YouTube videos, but he still showed humility."

—Hector Saldaña for MySanAntonio.com, writing about a March 2013 show at RodeoHouston

"...17-year-old Internet sensation Austin Mahone drew a rapturous response for his slick, Bieberlike pop. He's definitely one we'll be hearing more from – if we can hear him above those screams."

—Gary Graff in the *News-Herald*, writing about a May 2013 show at Ford Field in Detroit

While great reviews certainly don't hurt, Austin knows it's his fans who will truly propel his career forward. His may

Ab-propriate

Yes, Austin Mahone has been working out with a personal trainer, getting himself in shape for both stardom and dating. But his mom says those awesome abs need to stay under wraps – at least for now. In spring 2013, Austin posted a shirtless selfie to Instagram; within an hour the photo had 20,000 likes. Austin's mom, Michelle, made him take it down asap. "I get it," he told *Details* magazine. "My fans are, like, from 2 to 21. I definitely want to please the parents."

not have the largest fanbase, but it is an active one. When he posted a photo of himself and tour mate Taylor Swift on Instagram on May 4, 2013, Mahomies went wild. Within two weeks, the picture had elicited 218,000 "likes" and nearly 10,000 "comments." A few weeks later, on May 17, 2013, he took to Twitter to announce: "Ok....The day has finally come!!! I will be releasing the first single from my ALBUM!!!!!!!!!!!!!!!!!" Within five days, that message was retweeted more than 10,000 times.

"I love (my fans) so much and everything they do for me," the singer wrote on his blog. "They are truly the

Shower Time

Grab a towel and turn on the water! Austin Mahone admits he loves to sing in the shower (who doesn't?). One of his favorite freshen-up tunes is "Let Me Love You" by Mario.

FAME ISN'T ALWAYS COMFORTABLE

When fame comes quickly – as it has for Austin Mahone – it can be overwhelming. All of the sudden you can't just walk through the mall without being stampeded by fans; your time simply isn't your own anymore.

Fame really is the ultimate Catch-22. Singers and actors work tirelessly to achieve fame. Then, when they achieve it, they learn they don't really get to simply be singers and actors anymore. They are put on pedestals because of their achievements. Suddenly they're role models whose every move is being watched: where they go, what they wear, who they're with, what they say. They're scrutinized and criticized and analyzed.

Austin seems to be adjusting well, but when the lack of privacy starts to bother him, he doesn't need to look far for empathy and advice. Here's what a handful of other celebrities have to say about the downside of fame:

Country singer **Carrie Underwood** shot to stardom thanks to her appearance on "American Idol." Since winning the 2005 version of that TV talent show, Underwood has recorded dozens of hits and won six Grammy Awards. She says her road to fame has been a bumpy one.

"At the beginning of my career, I used to have panic attacks. People were touching me, screaming – it made me really nervous," she told *Marie Claire* in May 2013. "In public, I just get nervous. It's a physical reaction, feeling like the walls are closing in. The fans are great. It's not their fault. I don't ever want to come across as ungrateful. But on my end, it is hard for me to process. Because I am still just me."

Thanks to *Twilight*, **Taylor Lautner** quickly became an A-list celebrity and heartthrob. The young actor appreciates his fame, but notes there's a downside all his success.

"When I am traveling the world promoting the films, I say I am on vacation, but it's not really true, I guess," he told Hollywood.com in September 2011. "When I go to a beautiful city, I spend the whole time in a hotel room and then I am back on a plane to the next place."

Lautner said his busy work schedule no longer allows time for relaxation. He said, "If I'm not filming, I'm promoting ... I hang out with my friends, family, and kind of just – I don't even know. It's like, when I am not filming, it seems like – I don't even know what I do."

One Direction is the biggest band on the planet, but the strain of fame has ignited countless predictions and rumors about the group splitting up. **Zayn Malik** told *Fabulous* magazine that of the five guys in 1D, he's struggled the most with fame. He said online abuse against his family and religion has been particularly difficult to take.

Austin can't just play tourist anymore. Even his December 2012 trip to the Empire State Building was documented by photographers. Photo courtesy of AP Images

"I love the fact that I'm in a band, but it's very hard because of the type of person I was before," he said. "I was very reserved and just did my own thing. I guess I've probably found it the most difficult out of the boys."

The Hunger Games star **Jennifer Lawrence** told *Vanity Fair* magazine that she has more in common with her on-screen alter-ego, Katniss, than it might seem at first glance.

Like her character, she had a rapid rise from obscurity to stardom. And, she says, she often misses her more private, pre-fame life.

"I call my mom sobbing all the time," she said. "But (I'm) dealing with the repercussions of no more anonymity. You lose privacy."

best and most dedicated fans I know. Haterz can't hurt you unless you let them. And I just have one last thing to say.... Haterz gonna hate, Mahomies gonna love."

Ah, Mahomie love, it's a formidable thing.

Austin presents DJ David Guetta with the award for Top EDM Artist during the 2013 Billboard Music Awards.

"As a marketer, I know how devoted and powerful the Mahomies are," Charlie Welk, executive vice president of Republic Records told *Details* magazine. "You can laugh at the Mahomies, but they're serious. They're snipers."

Austin just hopes he's worthy of his fans' ongoing devotion. You see, this pop star thing isn't a passing fad for him.

"In 15 years, I see myself travelling all across the world, putting out albums and still making music," he said in a February 2013 interview on YouTube's Austin Mahone channel.

Of course, Austin knows he'll have to evolve as an artist to stay current; what works with fans when he's a teen won't fly with older crowds.

"For me, I'd say I'm going to go in the direction of whatever the hottest music is at that time," he said about future recordings. "I don't want to go in one direction and stay there; 10 years from now, music's gonna change, it's always going to change. So, I want to keep up with the music."

Keeping up or evolving into his own unique, one-of-a-kind sound? Only time will tell what the future holds for Austin Mahone. ★

Austin and Kelly Rowland team up to present an award at the 2013 Billboard Music Awards in Las Vegas.

MAKING IT EASIER TO 'GET DISCOVERED'

YouTube has become such a widely used video sharing website that it's sometimes difficult to remember life before it. The truth is, YouTube wasn't even created until February 2005.

In the eight years since it first debuted, YouTube has helped launch the careers of Austin Mahone, Justin Bieber, Carly Rae Jepsen and dozens of other singers, comics, dancers, broadcasters – and even athletes.

It makes sense, then, that *The X Factor* creator Simon Cowell and his company, Syco Entertainment, have partnered with YouTube to create the world's first global audition channel, The You Generation. Aspiring entertainers can upload audition videos for various categories, ranging from vocals to makeup.

Syco plans to determine winners every two weeks, and those selected will then become finalists in a global competition for a grand prize.

"We wanted to devise a way that is easier for you to get noticed. It's a simple idea," Cowell said in an introductory video for the channel. "It goes way beyond singers or dancers or all the stuff we've done before. And all the resources I have here or we have at Sony are all behind it."

The channel went live in 26 countries in March 2013; the competition is slated to go on for 52 weeks.

Simon Cowell attends a December 2012 press conference at CBS Studios in Los Angeles.

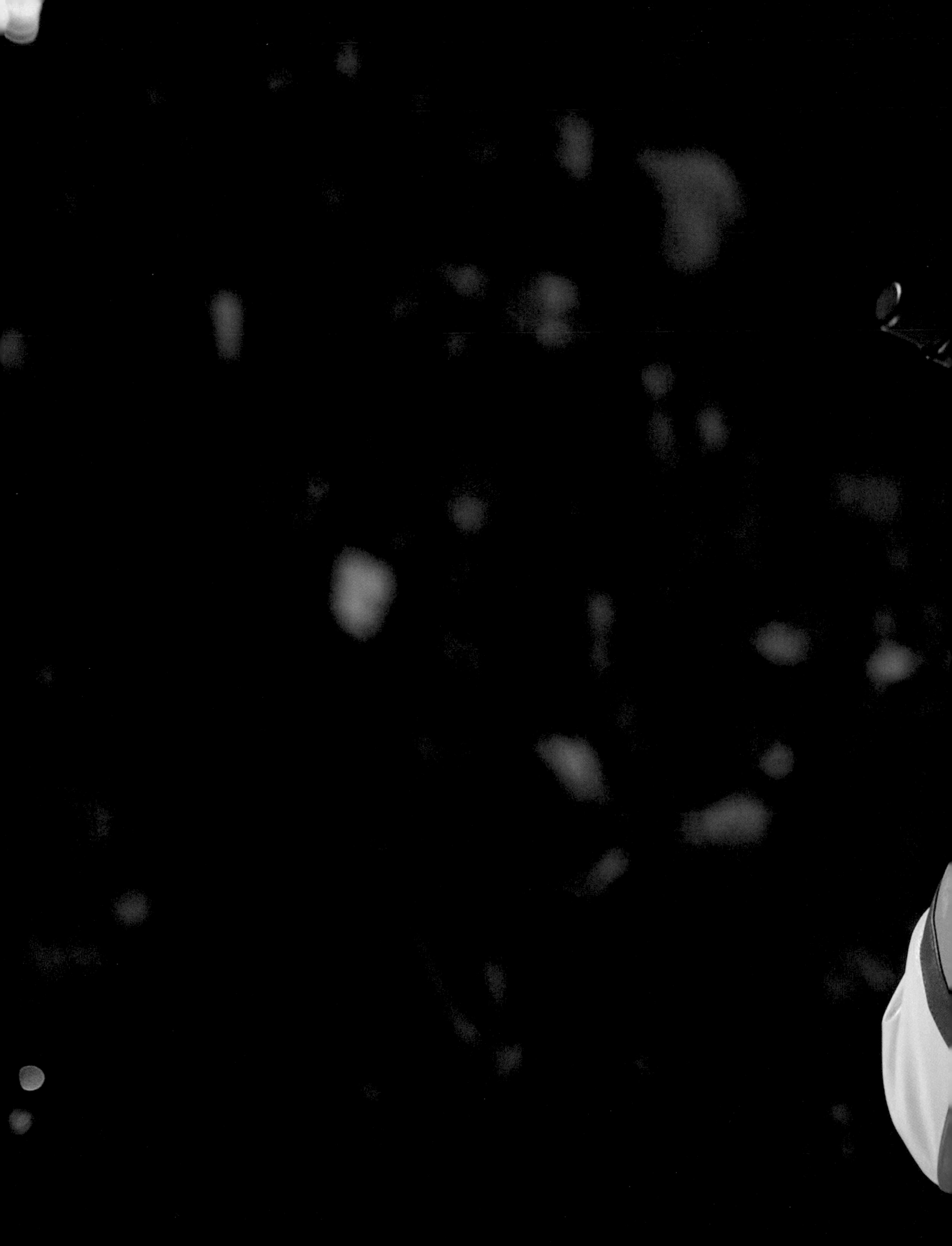